The Divan

of

Divine Presence

John Craig

Illustrations
by Kevin Watts

A Blue Logic Publication
www.bluelogic.us

Two of these poems, "Thinking" and "Dog", first appeared
in *Seven-Eighths Under Water*.

ISBN 978-0-6922161-1-8

Printed in the United States of America

Dedication

To Robert Burton: this harvest
from seeds you have planted

Contents

Illustrations

Introduction

What this book is and how to use it

This book is a large collection of poems derived from the experience of following the discipline of an esoteric school in the Fourth Way tradition. For purposes of order and artistic clarity, the book has been organized in the form of a single year's calendar and follows a daily and seasonal sequence. However, this calendar begins not in January but in September, moving from the harvest season through winter and spring to the full-sunned fulfillment of summer. What follows is a further, if still brief, delineation of the book's content.

Part I – Autumn: Gathering the Teaching

The first section is a poetic exposition of the ideas and principles under study and the beginning of a record of progress in the practice of the discipline. Esoteric schools, if still alive and not fossilized into religions or philosophical ideologies, work very deeply with but a few fundamental ideas. This book is focused on six such ideas, though it might have been as few as four or as many as twelve:

1.   God as the state of presence;
2.   Identity – the shifting meaning of 'I';
3.   The Work of Schools;
4.   The Steward;
5.   The Lower Self;
6.   Angels.

Some definitions and explanations are necessary here.

1. God as Presence

The purpose of esoteric work is to bring one's life to the present, a point not in time but rather the intersection of the dimension of eternity with the dimension of time and space. In his higher potentials, man is a unique creature, and his highest potential is that of developing a soul, a permanent identity in the higher dimension of eternity. Many conventional religions presume that one is already in possession of a fully flowered soul, but true esoteric schools understand that the soul must be developed through a series of steps or phases that require directed labor. The soul's completion is marked by a crystallization indicating its existence made permanent in eternity.

Within this context, God is not some external force, personified or not, but rather *the state of presence* one is seeking to find and then become. This may be the single greatest reorientation of thinking the book requires of a reader. What we call God is a state of being.

2. Identity

If God, the state of presence, is eternal, one's own earthly identity is a constantly shifting body of responses to stimuli we're mostly unaware of. In short, the pronoun *I* indicating self-reference means not one thing but thousands, but because we have a single organic body and usually answer to a single name, we assume ourselves to be a unified and discrete being. Psychologically at least, we are very far from unity.

Becoming unified is a crucial aspect of the work of soul development, an aspect that proceeds through observing the many elements answering to the name of 'I', and in that observation recognizing the distinction between the stimulus-response level and our more fundamental being.

3. The Work of Schools

The work of Schools is to foster presence and the development of souls. While the earthly appearance of Schools has varied, there are some defining elements. A School must have a teacher who has awakened and crystallized a soul and can thus lead others in that pursuit. Schools must offer an environment in which students under the direction of the teacher can work on themselves. To provide that environment, Schools will require a certain insulation from the common run of life, though students will come and go to earn their living and provide material support for the School. Beyond this, a true School can only be known from the outside by the results it produces in its students.

Without higher help (see #6), true Schools cannot come into being and develop. Ultimately, the awakening of the teacher, the establishment of a School, and the success of the School's ongoing work are matters determined by Higher Forces, and it is usually only from within the School that that direction from Higher Forces can be verified.

4. The Steward

If a different way of thinking about God may be this book's most dislocating demand on the reader, understanding the idea of *the steward* is the most structurally important demand. As already noted, a man in his natural state – his essence – does not have unified identity. In his social state, man's psychological fragmentation has been compounded by the creation of a social identity – *his personality.* In order to develop psychological unity, a man must begin to consolidate from within his being all the elements that want to create and develop a soul. To some extent, this is an artificial process: a man is under no biological pressure to create a soul; in fact, his biological imperatives can create a resistance. Further, his social and cultural entrenchment may make his personality quite difficult to penetrate.

A man must be taught by a master how to unify those elements within that want to complete a soul, and he must follow the master's teaching as a strict discipline over an extended period of time. The main source of energy in this work is the most intelligent part of the emotional apparatus – the part of the 'heart' capable of self-sacrifice, compassion, and service to a higher order. From this element, usually personified as female, is ultimately born a son, a steward of the house of one's being, to put the house in order. The steward is often personified as a heroic or prophetic figure: a Moses or a Jesus or a Muhammad in sacred texts, or an Odysseus or an Aeneas or a Rama in epic poems.

Thus the steward within is a virtual servant whose work is the refinement of identity. The purpose of that refinement is the creation of a soul, a project whose practical measurements are the frequency, depth and duration of the state of presence. The steward is not the soul, and eventually the steward must give way for the soul to realize itself. Moses cannot enter the Promised Land, and Jesus must die to make possible a higher dispensation. Despite his familiarity with Athena and his remarkable deeds, Odysseus is not an immortal.

5. The Lower Self

The *lower self* is the biological intelligence unwilling to transfer sovereignty to the steward. The term 'lower self' is broader than simple instinct, instead referring to all the elements both of biology and of personality that want no part of the effort of transcendence.

As making a soul – living in the present – is primarily an effort of attention, the lower self's most effective resistance is the disruption or highjacking of attention. It is the lower self that makes possible the seemingly harmless mental wandering we call imagination. But it is just this uncontrolled mental activity that seduces us away from the present and substitutes the intoxicating pleasure or the anxiety-creating fear that imprisons us in our heads.

As the steward is personified heroically in the literature of the growth of consciousness, so the lower self is personified destructively – as Satan, the serpent in Eden, the Sirens, or Claudius in *Hamlet.*

6. Angels

The instruction in true esoteric Schools does not originate with the teacher. Because the teacher is awake, he/she can receive communication from a higher order. Without assistance and direction from a higher order, the development of souls on earth would be impossible. The task is too daunting, the resistance too great.

In the context of esoteric Schools, Angels (by whatever name – Gods, conscious beings, ascended masters, etc.) are the crystallized souls who have survived the death of their earthly bodies. They reside above man on a chain of being, and as they were once like us, they are devoted to helping us.

However, their work takes place within a purposeful creation that must not be subverted, and their miracles are limited to a few at a time. It is a mystery how they choose who receive their gifts, but a true School is the product of their intention to concentrate the work of conscious evolution. An awakened teacher can establish an earthly form in alignment with higher purpose. Gradually students as they develop become sensitive to Angelic presence and will. At first, one is jolted by events and synchronicities even expansive definitions of coincidence cannot explain, but eventually one walks in their presence. While the teacher directs the School, the sacred work would be impossible without the abundant help of Angels.

What is most troubling for uninstructed men is that for instructed men Angels are not a matter of belief but of verification. In the religions, which are the after images of living Schools, belief has been substituted for being.

The poems in this section are instructions and thus run the risk of sounding too didactic to readers who are more interested in the aesthetics of poetry than in the growth of the soul. The poems in Part I are organized into fifteen rounds of six, each round representing the six ideas just discussed.

Part II - Winter: Youth

Once the tenets of a conscious teaching have been gathered, the long work of consolidating a steward begins. In the earlier phase of that work, its youth, a student will be both in and out of a new way of seeing and valuing, feeling the tension between exhilarating new perceptions and the resistance of entrenched personality.

It is a time of abrupt change and frequent confusion, a time in which one's growth depends on how willing one is to apply the principles of the teaching at a very personal level. The poems in this section are meant to reflect what a young steward would perceive and feel and learn.

Part III - Spring: Maturity

The poems in this section reflect the growing understanding and steadfastness of a maturing steward. It is a time of both greater stability and greater depth as the teaching has proven itself to be a trustworthy tool of the miraculous. As this stage develops, the steward can begin to confidently teach, as teaching is really only a more mature and responsible form of learning.

Part IV- Summer: God

Perhaps the last skill the steward develops is the ability to depart and create space for the higher state of presence to appear. In some traditions, this stage is more dramatically embodied by the 'death' of the steward; in others, the steward simply defers to the coming on of a pure, wordless awareness. As the state of presence – God – is wordless, the questions of how or why one would write poems about it are legitimate, but perhaps the reader will understand after reading that a poem or a painting or a piece of music produced with presence can invite presence in an audience. If you receive such an invitation, I urge you to accept it. It is the soul that experiences this state.

This book is intended to create opportunities in its readers. If you are a sincere seeker of a higher truth than you have been able to experience with academic learning, scientific study or religious practice, you may find something here. How to read this book? I suggest you read it as written, one poem a day over the course of an entire year. I would further suggest that you read each day's poem two or three times – in the morning, the mid-day and the evening – if you can.

You may find it additionally effective to read the book with a dear friend or two (though probably not more than two) who share your longing for something higher.

At the end of your year of reading, or perhaps before that year is finished, you could be ready for a School.

If you have already found a School (not merely a spiritually oriented group or organization but a conscious teaching whose receipt of higher help you have verified), this book will strengthen you and nourish your work.

John Craig
December, 2012

Invoking the Real You

It is not possible to be alone in Heaven, friend.
Divest your hoarded hopes, your secret thoughts, your objections
to creation, your fear of not being: remember God,
submit to the presence of God, the awareness of God,
the state of God—and here you are! And now the greetings come
from every corner of the cosmos right in front of you,
friendly waves from all the other residents of God's mind.

The body has been launched headlong through time and will expend
itself in time. Your custom tailored earthsuit gets wrinkled
and threadbare as its arc of time degrades. So what's the point?
I'm not talking to your body. I'm addressing that part
that still has a standing place in the next dimension up—
often called Eternity—the part that knows thoughts as thoughts
and emotion as a powerful function of the suit.
I'm talking to the visitor mindful of his earthsuit:
friend aware of your attention, these poems are for you.

Alive is the man who is aware of his attention.
What else does it mean to be? Not to be rich, to be smart,
to be unlucky—or to be a something, a husband,
a daughter, a German, a nice guy, a judge—but to be.
It is a shock to find one's body outside of oneself,
a thing in the external world, aching and worrying,
wanting applause, but there it is and here you are, aware
of watching that so personal parade crossing the mind.

The present cannot be in time: just try to measure it.
What is the present but a certain kind of attention?
What is the present but the state created by being?
Establish the present before you lift off the bedclothes;
again when your feet find the floor; again as your arms stretch.
Be aware of seeing the face in the mirror, aware
of your feet moving—hear them—to the kitchen. And let not
one untasted bite of your breakfast interrupt the present.

Believe your thoughts, believe that your emotions are more real
than your digestion and very soon you will cease to be
true to your experience. What's happening to your suit,
all the earthly tears and smudges, is yours to be observed.
You say, "So, suffering is not real? Tell that to Jesus."
Jesus knows, friend. How else could he put the cross behind him
and leave the sepulcher and become Christ? Believe your thoughts,
spend your wealth on your earthsuit, and to dust you shall return.

You get to choose from among the many things you can be,
the real ground of your identity. You can plant yourself
in some appetite or pursuit of comfort, in a skill
your hands or feet have mastered, or in some sweet emotion
like the love of men or dogs or fatherland. Or don't choose:
let the suit decide, as it will if you don't direct it.
The problem is, all these choices end the same way—dead body.
Only one location of identity gets beyond
the body problem: sit on the eternal perch and watch.

Autumn --- Gathering the Teaching

> *Is it such a great secret, what God, man, and world may be?*
> *No! But there's no one who wishes to hear; it remains a secret.*

Johann Goethe

> *Thou, O Spirit, that dost prefer*
> *Before all Temples the upright heart and pure,*
> *Instruct me, for Thou know'st; Thou from the first*
> *Wast present.*

John Milton

September 22 – God as Presence

The Three Conditions

We live in three conditions: Heaven, the presence of God;
hell, the absence of God; and purgatory, the labor
of mounting to the presence of God. The key to all this
is understanding that for man, God is experienced
as presence, a state that we can have within. To know God
is to be present; to be present is to be in God.
However, to be human means we fall away from God.
Turning toward and away, remembering and forgetting
to be, to hold God's presence: such is life in an earthsuit.

September 23 -- Identity

No Problem

I see you in your problem, and the problem is a lie,
a manufactured thing devised to take space between life
and death, so the you stuck within must also be a lie.
The solution? Don't be that you, the one in the problem,
the mortal one blocked from love; be another you, the one
watching the whole configuration curl and twist and form
and reform by the laws that govern it: What is watching?
Identity can move all the way up and back to God.

September 24 – The Work of Schools

Wanting

In the beginning it is good to want. Wanting drives you.
Desire is the engine of your efforts. What do you want?
Do you want to be wealthy enough to possess the earth?
Do you want to be admired by men, your worth acknowledged?
Do you want to be the stoic master of mind and flesh,
impeccable in virtue, impervious to weakness?

All this big wanting fades, over months or years, as you glimpse
the truth again and again. The stony, uphill climb burns
the silliness out of you; by the time you reach the top,
and you're free to have anything you want, all you can seek,
all you can know is the humblest, most innocuous thing –
the presence of God, always here for you to remember.

September 25 – The Steward and the High Heart

Madonna and Child

Let us attend mother and child, the heart and the steward.
Each of us is both male and female, passive and active.
Over time the womb of the heart is prepared, the great cup
of compassion forms within, and there the droplets of Truth
condense and accumulate. The male comes into being
as the need to act, to advance the heart's sanctuary
of understanding, and the son grows within the heart's form.
Both of them are within you, friend, and your most cherishing
attention – for nothing more deserves your best attention –
protects and nourishes them. What you were before fades out.

September 26 – The Lower Self

The Lower Self

The lower self is a warlord, you being its plunder.
It does not know itself, but it knows your captivity.
Holding you kidnapped is its identity. You're the one
who must worry about its death. If you are not conscious,
you become it, and when it dies, it can take you with it.

September 27 – Angels

Above the Author

Pink gladiolas shoot up from the vase on the table
before him. The dog sleeps curled on herself on the sofa.
The refrigerator's hum – ordinarily unheard –
vibrates in steady friendship with the silence. In his chair
sits a man with a bald spot, benign aches, a book and pen.
He has lived three-fourths of a life; he is writing this now.
He doesn't know who you are, but the Angel prompting him
may know. Heaven has its reasons why you are reading this.

September 28 – God as Presence

Greed and Joy

Strung up by overscheduling, we easily believe
the big deal to be real wealth, the party to be real joy.
With so much available, gluttony and greed become
a norm, a form, a part of expectation that conscience
fails to rule as the lone sheriff stutters at the lynch mob.

What is joy but presence, and while it can be amplified
by happy friends in comradeship, presence is the lone soul's
bond with itself, its commitment to its own true being
and sole fulfillment among humanity's noisy crowds.

September 29 – Identity

Perfume

Smell the flowers, but don't believe the perfume is the point.
The perfume is the reminder, the living metaphor.
Such is all the earth that you suffer and enjoy – a sign,
a thing to be in itself unbelieved, a thing to stir
remembrance of God, and you but that state of remembrance.

September 30 – The Work of Schools

Walking Upright

We all know the three conditions: being present, working
to be present, and sleeping. Schools specialize in molding
students into stewards whose identity is working.

The Angels take care of the first condition, measuring
according to their justice, which is incalculable
to us below. The world protects the state of somnolence.
The drug of habit is always available and free
whether one asks for it or not; iron custom dresses
us in clothing we must not remove, and the whole culture
conspires to degrade attention in mental wandering.

Schools refine the science of ascending from sleep to presence.
Few want that progress, and those who do need the sacred gift
of School to make breathing into conscious prayer, and effort
one's home address. This second condition, working to wake,
is what makes man walk upright and praise the presence of God.

§

October 1 – The Steward and the High Heart

Departure

The steward is the glory of the good earth, his suit cleaned
and pressed for the feast, the garment of virtue, the raiment
of devotion. Long, long days does the steward's growth require,
and when he is at last past refinement and free of art,
Heaven calls him to the staircase, the great ascending way,
and gives each step a name, and bids him mount this braided path,
this helix of thrust and surrender not found in nature,
and at the top the steward disappears and thereby breathes
the mystery, below which all our words inflate the mind.

October 2 – The Lower Self

The Fall of Man

We re-enact the Fall of Man a hundred times a day.
Adam's attention slackens just a bit, and Eve wanders
from the sacred place. The serpent, never breaking rhythm,
slithers up the tree and offers Eve a promising thought
which her vanity dwells upon. That's all there is to it.
Eve will believe the thought, and Adam cannot refuse her,
so out of the present they fall into the lower world
of doubt, good and evil -- all that. Now the snake is in them.
Eve's own tongue, talking away, is the serpent's head, thinking
for her, holding her Eye hostage in her throat, while Adam
begs her not to believe the thoughts she thinks to be her own.

October 3 – Angels

The Singing

Stuck low on every tree trunk, the husks of the cicadas
are the waste product of their choral rhapsody. Listen.
And this poem you're reading is the leavings of the state
liberated by the writing. The shade trees are nourished
by the dead matter, men by enchanting songs and poems
that with beauty prompt the present, sung by ones now Angels,
themselves sustained by rhythmic echoes of the Absolute.

October 4 – God as Presence

Attention

Attention is the soul's interaction with the body.
The lower one's attention, the more the soul is swallowed.
The soul ascends to freedom as will directs attention.
Awareness of attention is the soul's liberation:
presence – the dispensation of time by eternity.
Living presence is the soul's immortal art, not poems.

October 5 – Identity

The Question

So who are you really, and what do you keep from this deal?
What do you take back to eternity from your human
vacation? Not what you have here – it all gets recycled.
Oh, you'd forgotten eternity? It's easy to do.
Why do you think so many tourists come back? They forget.
Earth here is forgetting's most popular destination.
So who are you? It will not help to answer. Who are you?

October 6 – The Work of Schools

The Teacher

One starts with a shrine and finally builds a cathedral;
thus one man's vision can become a civilization.
Now that man cannot be a hermit. He must give his life
sharing the discipline. And the new civilization
will have the same heart as all the others past and future.
Culture filigrees the frame, but the picture is the same.
The sequence of becoming does not change. No God but God.

October 7 – The Steward and the High Heart

Turning the Heart

The heart requires disappointment. Too easily puffed up
with naïve hope, it loses itself in looking forward.
The world smacks you down, the smelling salts of humility
revive you, the chastened heart comes home. Now you can begin.

So what do you really want now that you're reduced to real?
It's funny, but now what's clear is the multitude of things
you don't want: shiny things requiring constant polishing,
esteemed things held aloft by fickle applause; mortal things.

Given the chance to be purified by intelligent
longing, the heart hones in on one abiding perfume, one:
God's own certainty, which can only be had in service
of the present, in the great divestiture of all else.

October 8 – The Lower Self

Closed

There's a pressure point at the base of the cervical spine
that can block the electric flow the brain requires to pray.
That canal held open, the tongue and throat relax, the eyes
move freely in their seeing, and the heart reaches the Eye
with its love embrace. The invisible Crown arises.

Close the gate and the starved brain can't know itself; it follows
a lizard's formula; the heart burns with zealous power
but no discernment, no sense of scale, no loving kindness.
Thus the fundamentalists who read the letter and kill
the spirit; thus the clear cutters who kill because they own.

October 9 – Angels

The Blessing

Once Gabriel did not address Muhammad for two years.
That I could not bear. But the Angels have not forgotten
my presence. Drowning in the flood or parched in the desert,
I'm brought back here and now by their love, brought back to the stair,
to the first step of self-abandonment, to the blessing
the Eye bestows watching the mind's boundaries burning up.

October 10 – God as Presence

Fit

The only distinction between you and God is rooted
in your desire to be separate. When you turn away
on one of your prodigal ventures, you would split apart
God to make yourself, but God won't be split. God can't be split,
so in imagination of yourself, you walk away.
When your silly little fit of self is done, you turn back,
clean yourself off, welcome in the one and only being.

October 11 – Identity

If

If you believe your thoughts, you will always be preparing
for the past. The content of thought has already happened.

October 12 – The Work of Schools

Sacred Game

Here's a game that will get you to Heaven: at the instant
of any kind of pain, trouble, trip, trap or confusion,
at the slightest slight, chagrin, sin, insult or suffering,
shift into the self-aware present and hold it, hold it.
The little torment will tingle a bit then pass, but you
will be here, the real you, at Heaven's open gate, welcome.

October 13 – The Steward and the High Heart

Son of the High Heart

In each new life, each labored arc of time, the forming soul
must make from flesh a loyal friend and servant, a steward.
The heart of man is the vessel, the womb for the steward.
In congress with the heart, the presence of the growing soul
fathers a son, a form in which the finest elements
of flesh consolidate – the desire to serve the higher,
love of God, friendship, self-respect, courage, humility,
patience, forbearance, the will to work with best faculties.

This son grows in strenuous devotion to one purpose:
the conscious transformation of worldly experience
into eternal presence, which is the growth of the soul.

October 14 – The Lower Self

Challenge

Most of our mind time is spent in daydream and inner talk,
indulgent arranging and worry: we call it thinking
because it seems to go on in our heads. But what is it?
It is the earthsuit pleasing itself – imagination.
It seems innocent to the world, yet it strangles the soul.
It opposes the soul's knowing itself in the present.

What fosters imagination? Nothing you want to be.
That's the point. The soul gets nothing from it; the soul's steward
dozes off, and the animal nature gets to party.
Remember that the earthsuit, though refined and beautiful,
is animal in origin and feels subjugation
from the steward's efforts in the soul's behalf. It's a war.

Only when it crystallizes as an independent
astral body can the soul live here without an earthsuit.
Angels evolved the earthsuit over time for the soul's use.
Still it overeats and blames its discomfort as excuse
to dodge the present; it drugs itself with entertainment;
and it lolls in imagination, snoring its challenge.

October 15 – Angels

Whatever You Call Them

You may call them Angels, gods, celestial influence,
conscious beings – by whatever name and by a physics
we can only know poetically, they've transcended flesh,
crystallized independent astral bodies, and live now
in the dimension of eternity – the mind of God.
Without their help, escape from the recurrent human wheel
would be impossible. They engineer the growth of souls.
These spirits were us once and wish us to become as they.

October 16 – God as Presence

Signs

Signals from Heaven are a great delight and a problem.
The soul loves communion, but the mind stirs to urgency,
interpretation, action. A moment absorbed in God
would have been enough for Noah's soul, but then came the words
and the blueprints and the Ark and the deluging terror.
So just know that when you're favored with a sign, following
will come a drama of learning tolerance for tempests
till you can bless the union of God's own terror and rest.

October 17 – Identity

Scraping the You Off

Plato suggested that each function – the appetitive,
the spirited, the rational – seeks immortality
in its own way. So one's actions are largely determined
by one's dominant function's agenda to avoid death.
Children, great works of art, comprehension of the cosmos –
all these are ways the lower self conceives of victory
over mortality. Thus brays the poor dying donkey.

So what are you? A proud parent, a master of some art,
a scholar? If wisdom is in you, you're none of these things
or any other things defined by an earthly pursuit.
To make a metaphor – and making metaphors is all
language can do here – you're one drop of God animating
flesh for a while. Thus you are – minus the "you" – eternal,
already free of death. It's only the "you" that must die.

Scraping the "you" off is a long and difficult labor.
Dismount from the flesh donkey and float behind it, watching.

October 18 – The Work of Schools

Practice

When you surrender to God and dissolve the false borders,
the illusion of I relaxes its grip on your throat,
and the Eye and the Crown are lifted on the flood of light
that had been hoarded below. If this is death, let me die.

You see, your illusion has built an electrified fence
around its imaginary lands. You call it worry.
You think that fence keeps out the marauders, but its real job
is to keep you unreal, an exile from the mind of God.

But as God is all being, you're included anyway.
Heaven and hell are both in God, but Heaven is conscious
of God's presence and hell is self-absorbed and locked away.
Whatever you want death to be, you must practice it now.

October 19 – The Steward and the High Heart

Claim the Heart

In tension, unease, worry, alarm and grim urgency,
the body registers every identification,
and the body, not you, locks up in imagination.
Keeping your earthsuit clean and pressed, unruffled and relaxed
requires a silent vigilance that's only possible
from an open heart, from a constant forgiving, from love.
From all the cramped, distorted postures of the body's dread,
you must claim the heart for your own, the all-forgiving heart.

October 20 – The Lower Self

Forgetting to Be

Just a quick shower – but the warm water washed him away.
She had barely begun the movie when it ambushed her.
While he thought he was reading the book, it swallowed him whole.
Predators everywhere – even the most innocuous
small activity can cost your life. Be on guard always.
Being must stand silently behind doing: the effort
to observe hails attention the soul can be aware of.

October 21 – Angels

Complete

As moments of presence are eternal, they are carried
life to life in a slow accumulating astral form
that after aeons reaches self-sustaining consciousness
and in climactic miracle crystallizes, fixes
as a soul complete, a conscious being, a citizen
of Paradise whose education is the universe
and whose mind is selfless extension of the Absolute.

October 22 – God as Presence

Pain

Pain keeps us honest. The earthsuit crumples into the cell
of itself and the mind locks out all imagination.
Against this aching and stabbing we must assert breathing,
delicately at first, then more deeply till we become
the breath, the simplest movement and rest, engulfing the pain,
swallowing the screaming nerves as food. Even here is God.

October 23 – Identity

Up

The burden of your manufactured self holds you down here.
See, in the mirror, the things you've assembled and put on
the basic earthsuit, all the customized accessories.
You can leave anytime you want if you abandon them –
scars and tattoos, firm opinions, affiliations, ranks.
Leave them in a little burn pile so you and the earthsuit
can climb till there's no more put-ons, no mirrors reflecting
what you aren't anymore, then no earth or suit, no down there.

October 24 – The Work of Schools

Movie

Take your body to a movie. Feed it some hot popcorn,
tasting fully one kernel at a time. As the show plays,
don't forget for a moment that you're watching a movie.
It's good training for watching your life leave the theatre,
get into your car and drive wherever it has to go.
Watch it. Don't forget you're watching it. You are the watcher:
the movie, your life -- don't get lost in the plot. Remember.
Eyes are for watching, not believing. What do you see now?

October 25 – The Steward and the High Heart

Heart Woman

The woman watching from your heart, speechless but feeling all,
must not be allowed to sink into anonymity.
She alone has the secret of your real identity.
Bring her forth, attend her, restore her natural color.
Install her as your prophetess. Listen to her warnings.
Humble yourself to her wisdom. She's your one chance to know
who you really, eternally are, O forgotten one!

October 26 – The Lower Self

Fine Fuel

When one is most capable of rising to the moment,
the underlord's slaves work extra hard to locate something
to worry about or take righteous issue with. What feels
so real in their anxious notice, that convincing alarm,
is the result of the fine energy they are burning –
precisely that fuel with which your prayer can provoke God.

So which will it be: churning thought trouble or your mind lit
by God's nearness, and perfect peace known by your hosting heart?

October 27 – Angels

Angels Attend

The Angels deal in suffering, death and destitution –
whatever it takes to loosen the lower self's clutching.
It is the lower self that blocks its own breath with worry.
Faith comes from enough experience with Angels to know
that your earnest work will attract the help your soul requires.
If in your trouble your soul knows itself, Angels attend.

October 28 – God as Presence

Here

Can you imagine a condition in which you are not
comatose but cannot reach the present? There's no such state.
If you truly want God, all the lower self's illusions
will dissolve before your effort to arrive out of time.
Subtract your ears from all the noise and you're already here.

To stay a while, hovering timeless in time, you must drink
from the cup of the heart and look with love upon the world.
And above you hovers God sending a blessing through you
to all you see. God and the blessing of love never leave;
it's you who wanders, forgets, makes a life of distractions.

October 29 – Identity

Not What You Think

I would ferry you across the river to golden fields,
but the boat you see is imaginary, and I am
not what you think. This is a poem, a small daily verse
you're spending a few moments of your life on, not a boat,
and you are not what you think. I love you because you've split
us in two and love is the only way back to the one
we really are, to the one God who is not what you think.

So jump in my boat so you can be sure where you are not,
and observe the distant hallucinated fields of gold,
and continue to think you're distinct from me and from God.
Eventually you'll grow tired of all that you are not,
here, past thinking, alone at the end of this diversion.

October 30 – The Work of Schools

Stop the Churning

Stop the churning, friend. Bring the scale of your life down to now.
Look! The mirror was invented to show you what you aren't.
Presence waits patiently for you to remember yourself.
Grip the cord of Allah. No matter what thoughts come, hold on.
There'll come a moment of emergence, a moment of truth:
thoughts will just be thoughts, emotions just emotions, not you.
Up you'll come out of hell, nothing but breath beyond breathing.

October 31 – The Steward and the High Heart

The Steward

We are multiplicities. We become a new impulse
every three seconds like lottery numbers popping up
on little balls that ride the earthsuit's agitated air.
17 – "I'm hungry." 8 – "I don't want to move right now."
39 – "My mirror needs straightening." 4 – "My head hurts."
Expand this mechanical action to a few decades
of moving around in the world, and one has lived a life.
The thousands of little i's which arise as responses
in here to stimuli mostly out there, each clamoring
to be recognized and so fleetingly called – these comprise
the lie of "I": I, the inflated tent housing this mob.

There's more to it, of course. The earthsuit does have a structure
evolved for us over millions of years. Incarnated
soul stuff attends it, aiming to grow and strengthen itself.
But the soul in the eternal present and the earthsuit
in time and space will not know each other and cannot make
a loving marriage without an intermediary,
a steward. The noblest part of the heart desires higher
being, and the soul reveals itself and breathes its blessing.
The steward is conceived and grows, transforming brutal earth,
governing the crowd of petty responses, directing
remembrance: an "I" more worthy and cautious of the name.

§

November 1 – The Lower Self

Prisoner

The lower self is criminal. It can pick your pocket,
an embarrassing inconvenience, or kidnap you,
hold you for hours blindfolded in a closet of belief
that the darkness is real. It doesn't want ransom; it wants
to hold you, to keep you out of eternity till death.

How do you know that you've become its long term prisoner?
Mostly by the kinds of thoughts you entertain: self-pity,
injustice, rebellion; the world (or your corner of it)
needing changing and you having just the insight required.
Your heart can marinate for months in these toxic juices.

Amazingly, the spark of God can still ignite your love.
If you are there in this dungeon, friend, this caved-in gold mine
of distorted good and evil, chained like an animal,
refuse to let your mind keep digging. Smell the noxious gas.
Lick and taste the cold stone wall. Feel your raw and swollen knees.

Start with the senses, purifying each moment, breathing
what is, and slowly, slowly mounting past the screaming gang
of thoughts to the door of silent invisibility.
Don't stop there: love is just beyond -- a long visit with God
which will restore the perfect pearl of real identity.

November 2 – Angels

Hoist and Harvest

What's it like to be an Angel? Yes, travel at light speed
(or no need to "travel" at all); yes, immortality
(identity without an earthsuit); but there's a big change.
You aren't "you" anymore. The thing you were – the agenda,
the secret calculations of advantage and loss – gone!

Because you serve God without impediment, you think God,
and whatever now unimpaired intelligence you have
operates keenly to share God – to reach a hand down here
(so to speak), midwife a laboring soul, hoist and harvest
another friend of God, extend the conscious creation.

November 3– God as Presence

Moving

The business of moving things around – rocks, dirt, crops, crafts,
animals, weapons, words, thoughts, stories, promises, money,
religion, prayers, radio waves, electronic pulses --
is what occupies men stuck in time. We move to avoid
confronting the fact that we're stuck, nailed to mortality.
The still soul observes and knows itself in silent presence.

November 4 – Identity

When I Was

When I was the body, I feared the death of the body.
When I remembered myself and returned to the present,
the death of the body seemed like a change in the weather,
a humid passage through a weighty overcast to pierce
the sunlit clarity. Fear and worry are the fabrics
of the earthsuit, woven tight to hold in a grim belief.
Don't get captured there, or here in this well-meaning poem.

November 5 – The Work of Schools

Schools

Schools seek to create an environment in which the part
of one that wants to work consolidates through use and learns
to foster prolonged episodes of the soul's awareness.
Too wordy? Try this: Schools accelerate the soul's progress.
They transform identity from flesh to the eternal.

From a God spark muffled in an earthsuit, one can become
an immortal conscious servant sharing the divine mind.
Schools lessen the lives required, shrink the wardrobe of earthsuits,
so to speak. But Schools are not made by men. Real Schools are run
by Angels: studying under them is rough privilege.

November 6 – The Steward and the High Heart

Man-God

The steward is the man-god or prophet of sacred texts.
He is Gilgamesh, Horus, Moses, Jesus, Muhammad.
He is the Buddha, Arjuna, Odysseus, Aeneas.
He is Confucius, Quetzalcoatl – a hundred others.
Whatever the historical truth of these great figures,
in the texts created by Schools, they are embodiments
of steward, chosen to communicate with higher worlds
and establish a new civilization's sacred way.

On an individual scale, the same drama unfolds.
Within the heart of each true student is born a hero
who will live to purpose and sacrifice himself to God –
the experience of God – the present – the soul's being.

November 7 – The Lower Self

Lair

The lower self has a hideout in the back, at the base
of the neck. It is a lair: there he cannot be challenged
or unmasked or repudiated. From that control room
deep into the mind he can reach; he can summon slumber
or wither the branches of productive thought. He can cut
the oxygen from breath, so that we turn to work with limp,
empty, downturned hands and dangling head. He can make all love
unprofitable and troublesome, unworthy and thin.

Looking out to the world offers no hope. No stimulus
out there is strong enough. You must sneak behind him, watch him
move his dials, send his demons. You must observe the mind
he's controlling. Only then will his thumb bone loosen on
your throat; only then will the wall crack in his airless room.

November 8 – Angels

Heavenly Conversation

Moses, Jesus and Muhammad were talking in Heaven
about mankind. Moses said, "Men are dead stubborn, stiff-necked.
Their stiff necks keep their hearts from sharing wisdom
   with their heads."
Jesus said, "Men cannot see past suffering. They preserve
the mortal part of themselves and forget the soul's estate."
Muhammad said, "Men want a God they can see and control.
To know and obey the invisible humbles their brains."
"And yet we were men once," they sighed in unison, "needing
the same eternal mercy we are stationed here to give."

November 9 – God as Presence

From, To

You can turn your back on presence, friend, but you cannot be
alien to it; it penetrates all the illusions.
It is here whether you wish to know it or deny it.
If you do wish to know it, just be aware of yourself
reading this poem, this breadcrumb left by God to help you,
one of a trail of them by which you can find your way home.
Yes, the journey itself is strange, confounding, frustrating.
It's the way of being and holding, being and holding,
till you harvest sufficient grains of certainty to make
your being and holding a joyous gift from God to God.

November 10 – Identity

Simple

Between the simple and the oversimplified stumbles
the human mind. Quieting down and not blocking the way
are restraints the mind resents, so simple being, the truth
of experience, has no role in the mind's churn and buzz,
its place taken by the dull, vague sense of something missing.

On the other hand, the mind starves shifting continuums
like gender into either-or formulas, fake choices.
Male or female? The answer is both, shifting and leaning
into the moment, though gender's not really an answer
to anything. The real you remains free of it – simple.

November 11 – The Work of Schools

Prodigal

The prodigal part of your life – the time spent impressing
other prodigals – ends when the accumulated truth
bears down so heavily on your false personality
that there's only breath enough for your infant soul, puzzled
at its own being, observing the world's strange self-troubling.

Yes, you must stop. A transition toward a transformation
must be made and held. You can mark it with ceremony,
distill it into symbol, but somehow under the Eye,
a pyramid – your new life – must be assembled, top down.
The Eye offers the earth the echo of itself – a word.

Be: a single syllable prayer sent on an open breath.
A priest, a steward, must be trained in the use of the prayer;
the word must become flesh and dwell in your feminine heart,
and the priest must convert your mind, both words and images,
to the lifting of the prayer, the remembering of God.

A clear labor back to presence, time buying timelessness,
an 'I' for an Eye: but if you think you can work alone,
you're still partying with all the other proud prodigals.
You're on the roof garden now, inhaling the starry night,
but soon you'll stumble back down to the den of loud talkers.

Just as you can't be prodigal but among the fallen,
you won't accept priestly discipline without priestly friends.
Returning to the Eye of God is more than man alone
can do; you must attend those ever praying the echo
of the soul; you must have the help of Angels. It is here.

November 12 – The Steward and the High Heart

Follow Him

Do not praise him. He is an earthly lord. Praise his maker,
the soul, divine spark of which this servant is reflection.
Obey him, keep his commandments. There is no other way.
His coming to maturity is a long discipline,
a straining in time to comprehend the sweet direction
out of time. Follow him following the strengthening pulse
of presence in the heart. He is the way back to the soul.

November 13 – The Lower Self

Not Lazy

Do not think the lower self lazy; it works tirelessly
to block and interrupt and siphon off the nourishment
to and from the Eye and Crown. Its self-importance derives
from the heroic stature it sees in its outlaw work.
How often is it tired, battered, aching, miserable
from the great battle of I versus the world! Thus the price
the lower self is willing to pay to keep the trophy
of identity locked in its coiled fortifications.

Thank God some morsels get through (God is the only reason):
aromas, tiny tastes of Buddhahood -- thus the Eye
reopens, its light flashes, eliciting, revealing
the ever hovering Crown, and God re-establishes
the certainty that I am a tarnished tin illusion
that the laboring lower self is clutching on till death.

November 14 – Angels

Me for You

The relaxed passive body sits in the chair and thinks not.
The soul is gathering from eternity things to feed
to the mind which will digest them and offer them to you
in these lines, measured and dosed for your heart's understanding.

You do not need me to remember God, but I help you,
and by following me, remaining aware of the back
of my head, you avoid the wasp's nest of uncertainty
and come more quickly to the edge, the point of taking off.

November 15 – God as Presence

Harsh Lessons

The harsh lessons are harsh because we refuse to learn them
easily. Identity hardens and consolidates
around an imagined "I," and all flexibility
is lost. In that condition, learning is very painful.
Love lubricates learning. It loosens the sinews needed
to kneel, to breathe God in and out; it worry-proofs the mind.
Whatever comes, whatever loss or repositioning
the course of events requires, God is here and would welcome
a hot relaxing bath in the tub of your grateful heart.

November 16 – Identity

Good Question

"Who am I?" you ask. Your question is profound, but I'll try
to explain. Please be patient. The answers depend on God.

When my mind wanders (and the vain mind will always wander),
and I'm proud and entertained and begrudge returning home
like a brat called at dusk to a dinner he doesn't like,
then am I the lower self, a fool hanging upside down
with my stupid smile of mortal amusement mocking God.

When I emerge from vain imagination in horror
at where I've been and immediately commit to prayer
and walk with that prayer the full distance home to God, blessing
my mother and praising my father, then am I the son –
mortal in a sweet way that urges God to stay a while.

And when the "I" – it's impossible to say – disappears
into God, then love arrives, here, dissolving all questions.

November 17 – The Work of Schools

The Friend Who Talks Too Much

He is your friend, also seeking Heaven. Do not allow
your eyes to look askance; do not grow impatient with him.
That he must talk and talk is part of his burden, the weight
of flesh upon his worthy soul. Find just the right silence,
so tiny it can slip between his rushing syllables,
and in it place your love, as in a nest waiting to be
remembered, recognized, reclaimed – a blessing for his soul.

November 18 – The Steward and the High Heart

If the Heart Could Not

If the heart could not overrule the lower self, the soul
might as well melt away. The heart is the scale, the fulcrum
making possible the ascent of self-knowing spirit
even as the animal nature dwindles and decays.
From the heart, wise in its longing and God-obedient,
rallies the thrust to move from dirt to sky, from flesh to light.

November 19 – The Lower Self

Sex

The earthsuit was made to produce an overabundance
of sex energy. Most draw from this great general fund
for vain imagination, for needless mountain climbing,
for needless fighting. So little goes for actual sex.
Like breath and thought and movement, sex is better when controlled
and intentionally focused, when God is invited to join in,
and love is welcome. Using sex energy just for sex
and God and love deflates the big unnecessary
bubble the lower self pumps up and occupies as life.

November 20 – Angels

Immortality

What is immortality? Awareness of God, that's all.
Across aeons we require finer and finer bodies
to contain that growing brightness – thus orders of Angels,
but each body has its end, and the eternal being
returns to merge its light in the awareness Absolute.

November 21 – God as Presence

What Else Is There?

Without God, all else is a thin, shallow consolation.
With God, all is a luminous unity of delight.
To be with God, to be in God, to be a part of God,
to come free from all the world's weight – all worry, all self-will,
to have all inner resistance to God simply dissolve,
to disappear into God's love so that every action
of mind and body radiates love -- what else is there, friend?
Are you tired of holding the door against God's pure being?

November 22 – Identity

Deep November

The foggy, leaden gray of deep November is a weight
on the mind, but strangely it can be an insulation
for the heart. To hug God close and confirm that nothing else
is necessary makes each rusting, surrendering leaf
a real thing, a glory. A dodgering wrinkled old wind
turns from the silence with a secret: "Don't believe your thoughts."
Thank you. In fact, I am the least poor thought unbelieved.

November 23 – The Work of Schools

Sequential Prayer

Cleanly prayed, *be* opens the portals from sacrum to throat,
and as they immediately would clench and close again,
hold holds them open, establishing control of the flow
which the *theme* directs and consolidates as attention
aware of itself. Then *back* is brought to bear, ambushing
the lower self before it can threaten the supply line.
Again the *theme* is focused, now at maximum volume
till the last gate cooperates, and the great Eye can *be*
in its own light, illuminating the four fold cosmos.
Thus flesh finds God who presides as promised, proving the real.

November 24 – The Steward and the High Heart

The Birth

The experience of presence inseminates the heart,
the intelligent heart not carried away by the world.
Pregnant with a higher understanding, the heart accepts
her earthly labor, to bear a human son of presence,
a mortal personality true to the dominion
of presence, a steward to move the multitude within.
This defining birth in our hearts we celebrate today.

Greatly anticipated, it is yet a humble birth,
a first fulfilling cry of certainty, a single note
of inner transformation issuing from purity
of purpose, from poverty of pride. Slowly the order
of the world will change around this figure. From the heart's house
he will walk in the work of presence, gathering allies,
spreading the influence of presence throughout our persons.

November 25 – The Lower Self

Dissolving

To abandon thoughts that would take control of the future
is to practice dying. The dark lord of the thinking state
has made time his responsibility and will cry out
that those who leave are traitors doomed to grim fatality.
In the truth of the present, one's pure awareness abides,
and the screams of the underlord and his minions fade out
into airy silence. The present dissolves the future.

November 26 – Angels

Sin Scars

Sometimes searing sins – "How could I do that?" – are staged for us
by Angels to teach us humility. Their bitter taste
seems timeless in meek memory. They keep us small and low
when the snake's arrogance inflates and so believes itself.

Snapped out of unawareness, we suddenly see or hear
ourselves committing stark cruelty to one truly loved,
and then it is inerasably done, forever burned.
"How could I do that?" Ever stinging hot, these scars abide.

The Angels arrange it all. They write the script, set the scene
and have everything prepared with perfect timing. Don't think
you do it – that's more arrogance. Nor is it accident
from which you can hold your cold heart blameless. Angels did it,
and like all their bright handiwork here on earth, and like "you"
and "I", their lasting marks can only be dissolved in God.

November 27 – God as Presence

The Absolute and God

About the Absolute, there is absolutely nothing
we can say, but we talk anyway because our concerns,
hopes, praises and beseechings make our fabricated selves
feel real in the relation. It's all imagination.

God means fundamental being, presence, a silent state
aware behind the cobbled mask of embodied selfhood.
Who is dancing where there are no names or designations?
In the light of God, prayers vaporize; gospels close and burn.

November 28 – Identity

The Book of Who One Is

When children finally sprout, come out from under the dirt
their parents have buried them in, they realize they are
their parents – bodies, minds – remixed and extended in time,
and those identities will move on to be their children.

Thank God that's not the whole story. The book of who one is
has another part – a reader. Is anyone reading
your life? Has your soul emerged to observe your flesh's plot
and see that who you think you are is just a knot of thought?

You can't be aware of what you're in unless you've been out.
So child, before your children bury you, might it not be
of worth to go beyond your parents' faith and hope and know
the soul, be the soul, reading this tale from eternity?

November 29 – The Work of Schools

Doing the Work

After a rigorous beginning, it is best to take
a slow, sure pace. Too bright a revelation could kill you.
Rather than the sun all at once, the darkness must be stripped
like putrid bandages that have come to hold back healing.

Your own personality will disgust you more and more.
You will come to see it as one layer on another
of thick varnish devised to hide the cracks and warpages
in your essence, to deflect the terrible attention.

Far better the life of the child still in simple commerce
with the country before time, the noose of pleasing others
not yet pulled tight. Better the ready insight not yet thought.
Better the unrestricted pulse of pure feeling, the love.

But it's not enough to let the buried child breathe again.
It is the incarnation, not the real you, not the soul,
and though the realm of innocent delight is dear, there's more
to be undone. Onward to nothing! The real you is God.

November 30 – The Steward and the High Heart

Heartwork

Why are you here on earth? Not for your mind. Your lonely mind
lives on a sparse diet of irony, sucking moisture
from foul weeds. No, the mind must defer to the heart, offer
the heart its bitter harvest. The heart is hungry for work.
It knows the earth's highest reason, the purpose of bodies.

Send your angry thoughts, your doubts, your judgments
    to the heart's door.
Let the heart take them in and work on them, crack and dissolve
their hard shells, free the misshapen kernels of love within.
As the heart grows its reservoir of love, it will alert
the Eye, the soul's pure sight, and the circuit will be complete.

Synchronized with the breath, the circle of love from the mind
to the heart, from the heart to the Eye, fuels the rising
to eternity, the unhinging of the conscious soul
from the body and the illusion of mortality.
Let the heart harvest sweet love and mill it to feed the soul.

§

December 1 – The Lower Self

Mindwork

Just as a country rots when entertainment has become
a major cog in its economy, the earthsuit's mind
disintegrates feeding itself on imagination.
The truth of the moment is blocked at the gates, breaking through
only by violence – your thumb caught in the door, your car
bumped from behind. The truth becomes something to be endured.

But we must do more than endure the truth. The mind's great work
is to hold itself open, silent, fasting, that the truth
may enter fully, unobstructed, and overwhelm us.
Such is the experience of God, and the work it takes
to welcome God is what the earthsuit must be trained to do.
If not working, it snacks itself fat on self-importance.

December 2 – Angels

The Human Form

"What a piece of work is a man," says Hamlet. He is right.
What would be a man was grafted to the tree eons past
and allowed to evolve until his upright readiness
to be the final host for soul plasma called the Angels
to their great project. Transplanted from the thoughtless garden
to the new artificial cosmos of civilized life,
man strives against his weapon-forging hands, his teeming brain,
and the heart-shrinking doubts of his own worthiness to find
his treasure, and in his best attention complete his soul.
Those who succeed – none do without help – the Angels welcome
to their ranks and put to work climbing against the current
of entropy back to the Absolute from which comes all.

December 3 – God as Presence

Both

Earth is a midpoint between the source of light and its end.
Both the blessings of divine presence and the mindless trudge
of zombie life are here. One has a choice of loyalties.

The presence of God does not make bleak December balmy
but makes the sting less important. You can be a body,
or your soul can use that body to learn what it is not.

The smell of death remains in the meat when God is cooking.
When the bright sun is dazzling the soul's Eye, pain is lurking
all round, working its way into every muscle and bone.

Love and suffering don't cancel each other. Not one. Both.
But bear this question: Toward which master leans your heart and mind?
Where is your attention now? Be with God observing it.

December 4 – Identity

Not the Mind

Are you in love with your mind? Do you marvel at its ways –
how it applies logic to problems, makes analogies,
retrieves experiences and abstracts meaning from them?
It's a wonderful if at times ungainly and sluggish
scout for exploring planet earth. But it lets you forget.
Does that pain you? Does what you've forgotten right now hurt you?
And what would that be? Why, the fact that you are not the mind.

The mind beguiles you into believing you're it. You aren't.
Aren't you bothered by that? And it runs on all by itself,
chattering and imaging, distracting you from being.
You must really love it to give it that kind of power.
Aren't you supposed to be in charge, monitoring the mind,
being aware of its function? As we speak, it woos you
from under your balcony, tempting your heart to elope.

December 5 – The Work of Schools

Suffering

Living on earth is hard; even the richest man suffers,
but through earthly suffering a soul can be crystallized.
First and constant is the struggle for special awareness –
the remembrance of God – and when to that defining work
true suffering comes, then first with acceptance and later
with embrace, one learns the miracle of transformation.

"Why do I suffer?" asks battered man. If your suffering
is mad and self-made, relieve it, but if your suffering
is intrinsic to earth, it is the opportunity
that brought you here to flesh and breath. Do not dismiss its worth.
The sheath of "I" must be eroded. One must learn to want
the moment as it is, God given, the coin of the soul.

For men on earth, God is a state, a participation
in the truth entered through the door of now. So hard it is
to want at all costs this state, this delighted selflessness.
So much must be abandoned to pass through, but having passed,
one understands the suffering: now one misses nothing;
the struggle to remember God transforms to God's embrace.

December 6 – The Steward and the High Heart

What Jesus Really Meant

Jesus said no way to enter the kingdom but through him,
and Christians since have defended their exclusivity.
One usual mark of a religion is its fierce claim
to being alone among religions, the true doctrine.
All nonsense of course. True doctrine is an oxymoron.

Religions exist to manage societies and keep
the great mass asleep. But then how does one come to Heaven?
One must consolidate the parts of oneself that desire
to be there and are willing to work. You'll need a teacher,
someone who has already made a steward in himself.
This is what Jesus meant: you must make a steward within.
He, Muhammad, Buddha – all embodiments of steward.

Having matured a steward – it will take years – you'll have learned
that Heaven is reaching down to help you, and you must use
that help faithfully whatever mess it makes of your life.
If you don't experience help, steward is unfinished.
Find a teacher already humbly breathing from Heaven.

December 7 – The Lower Self

The Bear at the Table

The lower self is a bear at a fine dining table.
It doesn't wait to be given a sensible serving.
It pushes aside the wineglass, napkins and silverware.
It dirties everything to claim it; it bellows and snorts.

But you may not kill the beast. You must accommodate it.
After a few anesthetic darts to slow its breathing,
it will accept a muzzle, claw guards, let its paws be tied,
take only the bites you give it, stop its surly roaring.

But you must be perfectly vigilant or back it comes
in full monstrosity to wreck the room. Such is your life
with this brute creature for the entire stay of your visit
to its planet. That's why you can't kill it. It owns the place.

December 8 – Angels

Beyond Believing

If seeing is believing, we are lost. Let seeing be
what your eyes are doing, and let the vibrations your ears
are collecting take themselves from noise to words and music
in your brain as you stand back in the wonder that transcends
mere sense, delighted at this earthsuit fitted by Angels
to your soul to help you find a home beyond believing.

December 9 – God as Presence

It's All Right

Are you disconcerted at the truth? Have you been naïve?
Were there hidden costs? Do not be bitter. That this is earth,
not Heaven, is as easy to forget as God's presence.
Things aren't supposed to be perfect here, or happy, or just.
Perfect, happy, just – these are qualities that inhabit
your soul – things brought with you. They are you, not things projected
on some earth claim. So what's the truth of your disappointment?
To condemn earth adds to unnecessary suffering.
Maybe you think if you're battered enough, you'll deserve God.
Friend, you can't earn God: you must collapse into the present.

December 10 – Identity

Still Here

You are still here. You keep trying to leave, but you're still here.
Haven't all your imaginary wanderings taught you
that there is no leaving? Only when you cooperate
with the here and now will you have a real life, a real 'I.'
If you try to sneak out whenever you get offended
or heated or just itchy or bored, your inheritance
of time will fritter away, and you'll experience death
as a foggy shade besieged by uncomprehending fear,
having forgotten that you're still here. There is no leaving.

December 11 – The Work of Schools

On the Ark

I see now what it really means to be aboard the Ark.
The mind lives in metaphor, a miniature of all
the social rituals, structures, habits and traditions
by which man makes a reality from reality.

When what man has made disintegrates – a cyclic event –
the Ark sets sail – the smallest boatful of purified minds
that can store the great harvest of the ancient ways, endure
the destruction, and come ashore as the next founding gods.

It seems quite plausible, and from miles out in space, it is,
but the mind of each member of the crew, a mind which must
command cold bellied panic to be still, rides in turmoil
on waves that annihilate all the metaphors but One.

The script for this drama is the old gods' grand finale
before they go on past human understanding, their love
perfected in the help they give. Without them, we would die
in madness, believing the flood, our minds drowned with mankind.

December 12 – The Steward and the High Heart

Focusing

Personified as Gilgamesh, Jesus or Muhammad,
the steward is really nothing but the constant practice
of canceling imagination before it acquires
any allure or momentum. The steward is not God,
but it can keep the mind clear for the present to appear.

The steward's task is daunting as the mind takes every chance
to wander away and squander its precious attention
in the theater of imaginary self. Loss! Loss!
So finely attuned the steward must be as to detect
each twitching muscle and firing nerve anticipating
mind's sneaking away – and to mercilessly block the door.

Dress the steward as you will – in Hebrew robes, knightly mail
or the habit of an abbess, it keeps the narrow gate
between the heart's distilling shrine and the mind's broad estates,
holding out the whores disguised as heroes while letting in
the tiny jewels of attention focusing the sun.

December 13 -- The Lower Self

The Donkey

The lower self behaves the way it does because its loss
of place and power is humiliating, and it knows
that its unspeakable mortality cannot be shared.
Do not mock it. Give it the comfort of a simple job.

It's a long way to Jerusalem (or any city),
and you won't make it over the mountains or the desert
without your donkey. It will fantasize its great conquests;
as long as you hold yourself above its dreaming, you breathe.

When it's refractory, be patient; when it's sore footed,
treat it with balm and beer. When maudlin in its memories
of when donkey's ruled the world, just keep riding. Use the stars.
Stay aware of your attention fixed on Jerusalem.

December 14 – Angels

Thank The Angel

The thought that all reality's just a spell we're under;
the small, sudden stroke of love unclenching strident worry;
the memory so free of time it makes a clearer now:
these small cracks where the light gets in are worth all the frescoes
you've painted on the thick walls of your solitary cell.

The amused certainty which observes the alien form
in the mirror, which understands that there can be no death,
which calmly refuses to join the urgencies barking
from every corner: this is the state of your true being.
Thank the Angel who has led you from prison. Don't look back.

December 15 – God as Presence

Open Carefully

Unique to humans are the apertures to God's presence.
They are of the soul – the Eye and the Crown – though the body
knows them as valves of a special attention, a brightness
of being, rare and beautifying, the summit of life.

Mostly they are closed tight, and we are bodies believing
the world, unmindful of God, fallen into plotting thought.
But as they open, the grudging corpse having accepted
the discipline, we are witness to the miraculous.

Be to BE. Full opening of these sacred apertures –
the terror and the love – destroys the illusion of "I."
We're not ready to be Archangels yet. Rather let us
attend the softest glow of God's presence for just an hour.

December 16 -- Identity

Observing, not Withdrawing

It is not the aim to abstain from life – its stickiness,
its thorns, its complications. The earthsuit cannot avoid
being stained and torn; and together, even only two
earthsuits, in hormonal heat or distant cold, will bicker
and bump for some rich exclusive dirt to roll around in.

If withdrawing from life could be done, doing so would slow
your progress. Better to not be the earthsuit, to observe
it conducting its affairs in its little arc of time
as your true being hovers and floats in the field of love,
its vantage beyond gravity and fear and time and death.

At this point, it's fine to laugh, even with a bit of scorn,
at what I've just suggested. That's what an earthsuit would do
in this situation, but what if above the laughter
you remembered your true self, your soul, and saw your earthsuit
as the thing it is, and could stay aloft in that vision?

Please remember yourself now. Be aware of your earthsuit
as not you. You are not its flesh, its agony, its loss.
You are the awareness lighting all that, a spark of God,
a soul observing the rich, tangled earth experience,
stronger for all the engagement you can separate from.

December 17 – The Work of Schools

Gathered

What there is to gather has been gathered. Repeatedly
have you been offered secrets men over millennia
have lived and perished to protect and keep pure. Your purpose
here on earth has been made clear. The present is all there is.

Don't close the book yet: make one more effort, one more turning.
Relax your eyes. Feel your back against the chair. Lovingly
stroke the forehead of awareness. Let breath go in and out.
Remember God now. The lower self rears. What do you want?

December 18 – The Steward and the High Heart

The Steward's Work

Don't mystify the steward. Its role consists of a few
discrete tasks which the soul requires of the body. Now hear:

The steward must tend and refine its own sincerity.
Though a warrior for God, it must think and feel as a child.
It must stand apart from righteousness and remain tender.

The steward must know the body, where the soul's nourishment
is stored and how it can be transported past the smooth traps
of the lower self. It must know how to staunch wounds and leaks.

By its own suffering (Again, do not mystify it:
to suffer means to accept the world as it truly is.),
the steward predigests to sweet compassion the soul's food
and offers it intimately, face to face, mouth to mouth.

And while the soul dines, its delight illuminating all
it sees, its witness growing in strength to stand on its own,
the steward backs away and turns to guard the narrow gate,
facing down the mob hungry to exploit the miracle.

December 19 – The Lower Self

Then and Now

Seizing the back of the neck and skull from atlas to peak,
the lower self takes dominion and lynches sleeping man.
The tension in the throat begins in the back of the neck.
The tension in the eyes begins at the base of the skull.
With the throat closed and the eyes glazed, the honey cannot flow
to the Eye and Crown. They starve. The hearts pumps and prays in vain.
Where is the balm of your attention, your friendship with God?

If you no longer talk to yourself, the throat will relax.
If no images move through the mind, the eyes move freely
in their sockets and what is before you is truly seen.
With the obstructions removed, the heart's sweet salutations
call the Eye to its balcony, and the vista rounded
to the horizon bathes in tender illumination.
Above the Crown levitates the inconceivable Truth.

December 20 – Angels

For You

I offer these words here as transformed things, born of weakness
observed, put down by an unsteady hand, meaning nothing
by themselves, but as they bring us to each other, making
a handshake across time, an embrace that bewilders death,
you can trust them. They confirm your soul, that peerless hostage
beyond hope with no interest in anything but being.
Here, aware, you are breathing the attention of Angels.

Winter --- Youth

> *I put your heart into your body for you, so that you may*
> *remember what you have forgotten.*
>
> *Egyptian Coffin Texts*

> *To make our way up to the upper air,*
> *this is our task, this is our labor.*
>
> *Virgil*

December 21

The End's Beginning

Cold sunshine and naked truth! Such is the end's beginning.
We wake up with the warmth behind us and need to relearn
the shivering dance we have tried for five thousand fat years
to forget. How fast the steps return! We knew this would come.

Welcome to the soul's December. Shovel your sidewalk clear
of all the plans you have made, all you have been working for.
The banks have shut their doors. The present perfect tense does not
mean anything true any more. All we own now is now.

In our desperate huddling for a shared point and purpose
is the seed of the next great age, not ours to see or know
but clear to God's continuing watch. There is nothing left
but the love of God and friends, mirrors of light to see by.

December 22

What Now?

Sometimes it is so hard not to give in to sentiment.
The heart is touched: the careful counted breaths of remembrance
give way to gasps, sighs and sobs, and the pleasure of release
overwhelms the meek steward's handhold on the gate. What now?
Even bankrupt, your true soul remains, and you will attract
new capital, new force, new helpers. Don't go into debt
blaming anyone. Praise God that your soul can yet praise God.

December 23

Can You?

If you want to come looking for the truth, you'd better first
clean your glasses. Even then, seeker, can you trust your eyes?
Who's telling them where to direct their sight, how long to gaze?
Is that brain of yours clear, or is it all crusted over
with a lifetime's habits, compromises, compensations,
noble lies and self-abdications? What gets into it?
Is it the smooth instrument you were born with before you
became the trusted you you've become? Can you monitor
the eyes' judgments and not believe? Can you observe the mind
thinking its way to its own version and leave it lying?

December 24

Simple

You don't have to do that much, but you must do it deeply,
sustainedly, and as often as you can. It's simple.

Remember yourself often and more often, and your will
to hold the state strengthens its duration. Hold it longer
and longer, and the earthsuit will relax its resistance,
and you will be more and more deeply your soul. It's simple.

Why would you not do it? Why would you not hold it and walk
right through the dismissals, the denials, all the nonsense
with which the functions respond, and keep walking on and on
out of the noise, out of time, back to God? It's so simple.

December 25

What Does It Mean?

What does it mean to be out of time? It means to locate
identity in that consciousness that does not erode.
The living present is in us. We must find it, be it,
and relax our desperate clutch on the noisy functions
that comprise our dear illusion of self. Let it all go
but the pure, irreducible awareness of being,
the mysterious now of attention which time is not.

December 26

One Choice

In each moment are many options but only one choice.
The choice is consciousness; the options happen by themselves
in the illusion state we don't have to choose. We must choose
consciousness, and again and again choose it, and again.

Vanilla or chocolate does not matter, not is it
ultimately important whether you marry Susan
or Betty, but it is crucial that you be here tasting
the ice cream, and that you are fully present to your vows
and to as many moments as you can accumulate
by whatever kind of theft from the mindless flow of life.

December 27

The Tools

He found the tools that those who'd escaped before left behind
and since then has been defined by them. He lives to escape.
He does not dwell on what has been lost in the bitter past.
He does not conjure a future of freedom and delight.
With some tools he destroys obstacles; with others he builds
bridges and buttresses. The doomed thousands who circulate
around the prison yard mock him, but he has found his work.

December 28

Normal

Return to Divine Presence, you prodigal. Your father
wants you back and would make a festival in your honor.
Now you eat what the pigs leave behind. Except for the dirt,
you are naked. What in you would choose this? Is it normal?

I suppose so, like thousands of baby spiders eating
their mother is normal. There are very few worthy thoughts
swimming in a human head. Most of them are piranhas.
Pigs, spiders, biting fish – you left the rare estate of God
to live a normal life among these animals. Return!
Evade whatever blocks your way. Let it eat something else.

December 29

Three Things

If the Higher Self is in control, abiding presence.
If the lower self is in control, imagination.
Neither are effortless, but they seem so because the work
sustaining them bypasses the will. All the will can do
is deliver one to the threshold of presence or break
the chain of imagination. So what are we really?

We are three things, two of them mortal. We are one third god,
not quite Gilgamesh. What your embattled will is doing
determines what this moment and the next will be for you.
Is your will climbing the narrow stairs to the square portal,
or does it lie hypnotized and idle in the dire beast's
rumbling tummy? It's so late, do you know where your will is?

December 30

Just Stop

The normal state of man is constant talking to himself.
By jamming the tongue into the roof of the mouth, we stop
the endless flow of words from exiting and being heard,
so others don't think we're crazy; but what's really crazy
is that we're all doing this all the time: thus it's normal,
as normal as all habits that waste life and buffer death.

Do you ever wonder what would happen if you just stopped?
Ease the tongue down, unclench the jaws, let the stuck throat relax,
let the eyes go loose in their sockets, let all the stiff necked
worry leak away and the love in the cave of the heart
come out to the light and show itself to ever present
God, who has been patiently waiting for your soul to bloom.

December 31

Dying

A played-out, saggy body can be cause for hopelessness,
or it can mother the understanding of deeper things:
flesh, time and what we are not. However it comes to you,
death will bring surprises, so having some simple knowledge
of what is dying and what is not is a wise holding.

Don't resist the dying of things that must die; mourning them
is ritual, not real emotion. These include your dog,
your parents, your friends, your body. Real revelation comes
when all these are gone and something remains – your true being,
the only thing you can offer to God, who will take it.

§ §

January 1

Just Two

At some point, when vanity no longer works, one must stop
to ask: Which do I prefer, wasting time or praising God?
That's all "I" can be, the lower self trying to feel real
or the steward serving with few words the higher order.

Imagination operates to please the lower self.
Prayer, rejoicing and renouncing operate to serve God.
Locate being: here now or there never. Seeking presence,
the steward works in two modes, just two, as the heart directs:
yes to God, no to plotting flesh. This is all men can do.

Simple yet huge is this teaching: it means the worthy part
of a man has no real choices except in the manner
of its worthiness in the moment; all else in a man —
his cleverness, his beauty, his talents and tastes and all
that he makes of them in documents and piled stones and heat—
belong to the forgetting world's unending need to eat.

January 2

Disappointment

Disappointment is a kind of cleansing, the end of hope.
The balloons deflate, the guests refuse your sugary cake,
the music gets tinny and bleak, the people drift away.
The heart remains in the abandoned yard, scraped raw and clear.

Disabused and absolved, one struggles not to waste oneself
in anger and self-pity. Against the sting tenderly
one returns to truth, urging the eyes up in gratitude.

January 3

Airport

For probably the sixtieth time in my little life,
I'm waiting in an airport for a connection, fatigued,
blank headed, out of my element, imprisoned in time.

This condition must not stand. I must concentrate enough
velocity of mind to be ready to leave, to fly,
so that when they call me, I will be worthy of their air.

This is what a man can do: he can make patient efforts;
he can be for lengths of time aware of his attention,
above the world of craving, floating free of his tired name.

January 4

Doubt

Nothing clings more tightly than nothing made something by doubt.
I can't tell you not to doubt without your doubting growing.
When doubt is the currency, you can only buy something
not happening and not worth it, so your doubt should be saved
for the things you really don't want to be in your presence.

January 5

Insurance

I want to buy kidnapping insurance, but I don't know
who the kidnappers are. Each time they take me, I wake up
later somewhere else, shaking off fuzzy uncertainty
and brain jamming confusion, knowing that I am here now
but was not and not knowing who tricked me or what they took.

I want some protection, but the insurance brokers say
the kidnappers could be anyone, and one can't protect
against just anyone. Besides, they add, how could they know
I wasn't scamming them? My claim could be a clever fraud.

Perhaps, they say, I only want money, not to stay here
undisturbed by those thieves whose sole target I seem to be.
Who are they? What do they really want? Where will I wake up
tomorrow? Here, gone, here. Who can live this way? Can you help?

January 6

Gallows

How did you get up there on the gallows, friend, your hands tied,
someone behind you mouthing a prayer while a few dozen
stand around with their eyes locked down? This is your life. Tell me
why you are living it as a prolonged execution.

You can slip the noose of this version of yourself. You can
simply step back in heart and mind and at last in full soul.
Very quickly someone else will be found to take your place.
Humankind does not need you to die, not you, just someone.

God is always here waiting for you, but you must be God
to be welcome in God's arms. You must be what a soul is.
The fragile trap door beneath your feet keeps creaking. Let go
of this felon's life, this bound, guilty, what-have-I-done dream.

January 7

Wrestling

Is my life really a wrestling match with the lower self?
Yes, but only if I'm not content to be his captive,
a model prisoner, taking what I'm given, lying
about my efforts and my states. Only when I fight him,
use my will's weapons, do the glimpses of what I'm missing
bind together into a life hospitable to God.

January 8

The Buddha's Right

The Buddha's right: it's a problem that we think we have time.
But what's worse is to think we are time, and that's what I do
whenever I attach the word "I" to the earthsuit's life.
It breathes, eats, moves things around, talks, thinks, hopes and imagines
as what I truly am holds open presence eternal.

January 9

Don't Do It

Don't kiss the girl thinking you're in control. Another kiss
is all you'll want, and for it into the desert you'll go,
following her fleeting form, losing your bearings, straining
your eyes. "There she is – to the left – faster. I'll have you, girl."

When you finally come to, your nose and mouth full of sand,
you'll feel like a fool, justly so, and if God did not love
you so strongly and did not want you back in Heaven now,
Angels would disdain this poor man seeking love without God.

January 10

Real Life

Your body is an instrument evolved for a purpose.
If you don't use it – master the skill of it – the body
imagines an identity for a span and then dies.

Let the body be the object of your observation:
note its functions and behaviors, but don't believe it's you.
Keep a distance. Let that presence that can watch the body –
including its feelings and thoughts – grow stronger by this work.

This awareness must be remembered moment to moment,
or the body pulls you back to imaginary life.
You, aware observer struggling to be, you are real life.

January 11

Ablution

Wash, wash the dust that every day blows in to mar the light.
Clean the mind again, again. So quickly loosens the grip,
and we slide away into the lies of mortality.
Only high up, up very high, is the air truly clear.
Go higher, above the air itself, beyond the last thought,
to the very edge of mind. Now new, cross into silence.

January 12

All You Do

Being in the state of God, submitting life to presence,
is compatible with every tiny worthy labor.
Sweep the walkway, change the bulb, offer the birthday greeting,
comfort the sick, advise the children, look, hear, feel, move, talk.
Be the emissary of presence, as one with a soul,
and the burden of "I" will lighten to near nothingness.

When you drift and wander into the unnecessary,
accident governs your actions, and poorly stitched belief
is your only clothing. You can be in the dark for hours,
fumbling for light till a lucky shock restores your one choice.
Ah, there you are again, doing whatever you're doing,
returning the world breath by breath to the presence of God.

January 13

God in Bodies

We are God in bodies, and the only way I make sense
is by being that which climbs to the bright fatal threshold.
I mount the staircase, each measured step further from my flesh,
take the last long surrender into air, and God is there
where I no longer am. God has left the body of me,
like the ocean poured out of a jug, expansively free.

January 14

The Present Nothing

A promise fulfilled, the opening of a ripe melon –
such is the instant of elevation after the prayer
has come to be loved for itself and is no more a means.
You see, the state arrives when you no longer desire it
because only then is there empty space for it to fill.
Desiring to be close to God is only the first spark
of becoming the purified now, the present nothing.
Be nothing, want nothing, nothing: in no time God is here.

January 15

Betrayed

"That was so good," said the mouth with words from the willing mind
as the fine morsel descended into the wakened snake
which urgently dashed off a nerve mail to the brain which dropped
another word into the throat for issuance forth: "More."

The cycle repeated till all involved lost count and slowed
into torpor. "Son," said the heart mother, "where have you been?"
"My God," said the son, "it has happened again. Where was I?"
"Dear," said she, "you were betrayed again by a trusted thought."

January 16

Breathing

Breathe in, breathe out. The birth of being and the death of doubt
enact each breath, each warming of the heart and quieting
of the self-amusing mind. Exposed by the cleansing prayer,
the deathless part presides, commands the body not to slink
back towards sleep but hold open to God the ascending spine.
Look up! Up! The dirt will have its part soon enough. Look up!

January 17

Hold and Feel

The lower self is a superb sneak thief; that we all know,
and we have learned to watch for his tracks on the assumption
that he is watching us and waiting for our slightest lapse.
But there are also times when he is quite brazen, brutal
in his bold assertion. He'll make you sick, he'll make you faint,
he'll make you choke and cough and flee for air at the summit
of a sacramental effort. And having forfeited
the opportunity for prolonged presence, suddenly
you'll find that the nausea and the rude coughing spasm
have abated and you're fine. You return stunned and chagrined.

How does one work with this delinquency? Feel the deep sting
of each whole cough; feel the fainting rush; feel the collapsing
porch of your stomach; feel all of whatever he's doing
and hold the rope. Turn the beam of presence on his mischief.

January 18

Please Come In

Excuse me, please. I require your help for just a second.
Would you hold the door while I enter the present? Thank you.
It's better here. Your simple kindness won't be forgotten:
just remember yourself being here with me. Still holding
the door open? Please bring yourself in. You must go, you say?
I assure you, it's better here. All your obligations
have already moved on, light years ago. They don't miss you.
All the people pass by heading somewhere they imagine,
but step in and you'll understand: being here is better.

January 19

What the Lower Self Wants

It's not the money or the sex: what the lower self wants
is not the commodity but what that means to the lie
of its existence. And then there's the compulsion itself,
the adrenal mania so far from the love of God.
To forget such love closes the sky, as forgetting God
locks one in the corpse that must eat too much and drive too fast.

January 20

Rushed

The illusion of being rushed is one of Satan's tricks.
Of course you don't have time, nor do you want it. The present
is not in time but in attention. If you are aware
of your attention, time and its debris – so dear to him –
float on under the bridge you watch from. What is feeling rushed
but the lower self kicking the walls of his labyrinth?

The body exists to feed you, my darlings, to nourish
your presence. Your faithful servant directs your food's passage
from the great refinery up the precarious steps
to your gate and thence to your table. All time is for you.
Do you remember? The enterprise of flesh was fashioned
for you. It it feels rushed, learn mercy from its suffering.

January 21

Get to It

Hasn't this gone on long enough? Can you not calculate
life without this cycle of petty helplessness. God's gift
is put on hold waiting for your will to exit the tent
and line up your forces. If you're afraid of victory,
say so: your next step will be directed, and then your next,
but if you're just lazy, hell will harden all around you.

January 22

Talents

How does one give up one's talents to God? Piano keys
may produce poignant marvels under your fingers, golf balls
leap off your club toward the stratosphere, stocks and bonds beckon
you to their hidden wealth, or poems in profusion rise
from your brain like butterflies. All lies. Mere capacities
of your earthsuit. Don't trust me, check the rental agreement.
Find the model number and the date of manufacture.
Cross-reference them to 'talents.' You'll see them: everything
you can do on this planet for as long as you've paid for.
Let them go. God prefers you when you don't hide behind them.

January 23

Good Morning

I'm not trying to change you – far too big a job for me.
Besides, changing you is robbing you of your capital,
the hoard of falsehoods and old attachments you'll need to burn
to forge a soul. You have to do your own bodybuilding.
I'm just here to announce the morning and get a sweet chant
started in your heart. Then perhaps we'll take a walk, find God
shopping at the bazaar, and note which fruit God's mouth savors,
holds in delight. We only want what's for God's own table.

January 24

Florida

One reason for a trip to Florida is you might see
a blimp in the sky. We're too impatient and too blinded
by urban glare to actually observe the movements
of Heavenly things anymore, but beholding a blimp
in its almost deniable progress can put a hold
on the fast forward urgencies of our machinery.

Also, there are a lot of old people in Florida.
Their slow driving can help you. Instead of trying to pass
on the left, get to the right behind an aged creeper
and watch patiently for this swampy state's only exit.
You may feel your readiness slowly inflating with love,
and up you'll go, flying slow enough for earth to doubt you.

January 25

What Can a Man.......?

What can a man give to a woman who does not need him?

No higher joy for me than her attention, yet she comes
to the window so rarely, and her gaze is so fleeting.
Some magic I must employ, a spell or incantation
with a power greater than her self-reliance. What key
can unlock the love that must be there, for only love
can be so self-content? She is not of this dimension.

What stall in the bazaar can sell man the map out of time?
Where is the carpenter, where the tools to build a ladder
high enough to reach her window? No God a friend to man
would make this longing without offering a way to quench it.
Here my cry, Lord. I am in the prison of my own heart.
Teach me the strange singing her attention cannot resist.

January 26

Shoes

Be careful with your certainty. Keep it under your hat.
The loud woman, wherever in the house you let her live,
regards a higher state like a new credit card; hide it
before the stores open or you'll trade presence for lipstick,
an ostrich skin handbag and the cutest little earrings.

She can't understand. For flesh, finding twelve hundred dollars
in the street is thrilling. How hard it is to invest it
in more time with God. One can't know when God will be back through,
and in the meantime, one has to hold up the starry sky.

But when she comes barging in, ignore her. She'll whine and cry,
"I need them. I need those elegant shoes." Tell her her feet
are beautiful, though she'll scream, "To hell with feet. I need shoes."

January 27

The First Step

The first step is surrender, but the young, their sap gushing
over the highest dams, must rebel. They can't yet distrust
the gleam of their thoughts and the symphony of heart and blood.

The soul grows by accepting: that's why again and again
it comes to beautiful, battering earth – to feel the blows
and breathe the ecstasies until they're one seamless garment
of awareness worn before God. Thus dressed, the soul can leave.

But the young, frolicking, feeling their power, expanding,
amazing themselves with sex and knowledge and sure conquest,
caressing their self-importance, how can they not believe
all of it, which the soul must absorb, contain, neutralize
in self-aware abeyance? How can they not? The first step...

January 28

The Lilies of the Field

Instinctive pressure – food, money, fighting, sex – sweeps away
the heart and head and drowns the hope of poetry. Choose now
before the urgency finds an action and the earthsuit
inflates to full forgetfulness. The lilies of the field,
so easily trampled, impossible to trust, must be
the heart's harvest – longed for, located, approached, gazed upon,
confirmed and recorded to the rhythm of conscious breath.

January 29

Let It Go

When you make a mistake, note it and let it go. Don't try
to chase the thing down the Karmic road: you're not fast enough.
Angels have many duties to carry out; one of them
is to construct opportunities for us to pay debts,
so be ready. When you encounter a friend who owes you –
perhaps an old slight or an omission – greet him with love.
Help the Angels. They speed ahead preparing our good luck.

January 30

Its Pleasure

The lower self takes its pleasure in deceit; the alarms
it sends are often lies, not because there is no danger
but because there's nothing we can really do about it.
If the sky falls, we're all doomed, but if we believe the sky might fall,
we defer to Mr. Gut, who mounts the bridge, spreads himself
in the captain's chair and proceeds to waste the next few hours
on what-if scenarios and/or imagined triumphs.
Mr. Gut's version of life? Rule by controlled illusion.

January 31

Till Then

Unfathomable as it is to you, God's creation
takes care of itself; when you are God, you will understand.
Till then, your job's simple and clear: quiet presence. To be
means to remember yourself now, to witness self-aware
the drama of your own becoming. The events go on,
your flesh takes part, but you must go above events – deathless,
invisible, certain – by love expanded into God.

§

February 1

Winter

In winter one puts on layers of clothes and still shivers.
The body does not understand. It only strategy
is to keep adding things on. More fire, more fabric. More, more.

There is another way. One can be less. In fact, the less
one is, the more available is God, and the presence
of God transforms the body into a rough otherness.

The tiniest candle, the servant of becoming less,
will confound the body, displace its strategy of more
with the starry quest for nothingness, the garment of God.

February 2

Thinking

There I go again thinking about the future. I know
it's silly and useless, a waste of mind time, a secret
pandering to vanity, but thinking about the past
is just painful, and thinking about the present – try it –
you'll see it just can't be done. I mean, you can remember
the present, but you can't really think about it: you keep
bumping against the wall of this damned dimension, a fly
banging the window unto death. So what to think about
if not the past, present or future? Must I abandon
thought here by the roadside and locate myself by the stars?

February 3

The Divine Labor

You are falling in love with this teaching; this little bit
you have sampled fires the heart and urges you past the mind.
The problem is, it's worse to dally with this instruction
than never to have met it at all. You get a few weeks,
a slow warming; you delight in the discovered present,
you surge in the elation of knowing life's true purpose.
Perhaps an Angel visits and pours on your head a dram
of God's presence and the cognitions of eternity
fly like bright sparks. Yes, you have found it. It is real. Now what?

The divine labor begins. Take a step out of the fog
you've been raised in, only as far as certainty allows,
a step you know you won't retract. The process of dying
and that of striving are simultaneous, intertwined
as the twin snakes of transformation measure their ascent.

The next step confirms the first, holds open the blessed door.
No dawdling now. Be aware of your attention and step,
then straighten your back and firmly step again. The final
assertive surrender takes you aloft, breathing Heaven.
This ritual is a microlife, to be repeated
as long as flesh clutches you down to time: brief discipline
of a strengthening soul, training to bear the miracle.

February 4

Vanity

Standing naked before a crowd of strangers confessing
your darkest secrets – even this the lower self will turn
to vanity. No ritual, no ridicule renders
it helpless to lick your ear and whisper its advantage.

You must fill your heart with the labor to remember God,
and as what you listen to captures the heart's attention,
the words you say to yourself must be true prayers, directions
in God's own syllables, protecting your humility.

February 5

The Sleeper

His sleep is not rest. It is a collection of postures,
a repertoire of clichés, a program of thoughts moving
sluggishly through time unaware. It is the only life
most humans practice, and it is the sleep of no waking.

His knowledge has no truth. It is a balloon filled with facts,
traditions, habits of mind and firm belief held aloft
by everyone's participation. It can't penetrate
the mystery of being, but it fascinates his sleep.

His love has no soul. It guards the borders, protects the house
and family, observes the gifting days, takes its pleasures
lawfully and cleanly, grieves loss credibly, and feels sure
that heaven will welcome the people not guilty of wrong.

His God is not God. His is omnipotent, omniscient –
all the omni words – and it abides in churches, temples,
mosques and wats where sleepers pray the prayers to keep fear alive.
"In obedience to you, my Lord, let my sleep go on."

February 6

Which Will You Be?

Which will you be as you read this – animal or Angel?
Will you decode the words grudgingly, yawning and yearning
to return to the vagrant stream of self-indulgent mind,
the unlaboring life of those deteriorating
into dead matter? Very well, stop reading. Back to sleep.

But for you few who prefer the wonderful suffering
of transformation, you who would create souls of yourselves,
feel the fire of the words in your mouth, their sweet smoke rising
to cleanse your brain, dispelling all the fat, chattering thoughts
that had you convinced of their value. Now you are empty
and God can come and install a perfect presence in you.
Now, Angel for this moment, start a life of permanence.

February 7

Greed, You

The cost of greed is your idiotic wobbling around
under the weight of what you've seized and refuse to put down.
At some point you'll topple and all the stuff will fall on you,
and you'll want to trade it all for one clean, fully felt breath.

Your mind is like a river in flood, but instead of cars
and bicycles and bloated pigs and furniture and trees,
what surges on the current are the logics and the lies
and the promises and the plans that hold identity.

And you keep adding to the glut, acquiring unto death.
You are greed: gross, clutching, toppling, swept off, drowning in mind.
Drop it all. Try to make your way to shore. Pull yourself up,
drenched, naked and exhausted out of thought: breathing, breathing.

February 8

The Human Thing

Just on the other side of this curtain of vanity
is the silent universe of love. Why do I stay here?
Because I cannot do otherwise. I only exist
on this side of the curtain, and if it were to open,
I'd be annihilated in an ecstasy of truth.

So instead I stay back here and do the whole human thing.
I tell jokes to myself. I map my kingdom. I believe.
My invention of the mirror was a huge step forward
for my security, as if the curtain were sewn shut
and my own audience appeared wanting my attention.

Still on occasion a solar wind stresses the fabric
to its ripping point, and I feel myself disappearing.
I shouldn't say this, but the terror of it is thrilling,
and the prospect of coming face to face with whatever
God is holds me in pure surrender till the gust has passed.

February 9

Authority and Power

Whether the chairman gives an order or the pope issues
something infallible, the only real authority
comes from our own recognition of truth in what's expressed.
The rest is merely power and means nothing to the soul.

Authority is the communication of being,
and because the Lord our God is one, we are reminded
to be whenever true authority is detected,
whether in words of the Teacher or any other source.

We must honor the reminder to be, to go deeper,
to return to God, and be grateful to the messenger
whether he's singing or cracking a whip, and when you must
kneel to power, let your soul's authority bend your knee.

February 10

What Prayer Must Do

Prayer must sustainedly interrupt imagination.
To do so, it must be rhythmic enough to be fluent,
and fluent enough to be unceasing, yet so distinct
in its syllables that the will can hold and carry it.

God does not require our words, our incantations and spells.
God is always here but shadowed by the thick intrusions
of the lower self, a curtain of clouds between the earth
and the constant sun. God does not need our praying, we do.

Our prayers thrust through the clouds and reveal the sun, penetrate
and dissipate the lies we have been lured to imagine.
When the Eye of Heaven clears and we know ourselves to be
none other than the light of God, prayer retreats to silence.

February 11

The Real Reason

Morality teaches you to cultivate compassion
so you can palliate the pain of others. Fair enough.
Morality is reasonable but not real reason.
Earth pain is irrational, endless like the number pi
and meant to be that way. If you relieve it in one place,
you create it in another. If you could end it all,
you'd waste the Angels' genius. Relieving suffering
is one of the heart's capacities, but true compassion
has a higher purpose than feeding the starving children.

Feeling what another feels requires you, for an instant
or an inch, to separate from the teeming cloud of thought,
desire and urgency you have made into reality.
Shocked at your brother's wound, your heart moves to the threshold's edge,
from where your soul can see light and remember true being.
If all you want from compassion is a lump of goodness
to give your lower self a sugar high, then you'll get it.
But you don't get it. Your compassion defines the border
of what you are not, where your soul can know itself and God.

February 12

Two Different Kinds

If your toothbrush made the noise of a jackhammer, your sense
of scale would be confounded; likewise if the lion's mouth
gaped wide to squeak. So how bizarre it is to remember
the lyrics of a song for decades and forget God now.

Of course we're dealing with two different kinds of memory –
the rhythmic repetition we employ for reciting
and the remembrance of Allah which snatches the present
from the flow of time and bestows on us the here and now.

Still, memory follows attention, and the greater scale
of remembering God, of waking the soul with the breath,
must not be confused with the beat of a rock song pounding
its rhythm into pelvic recognitions in the brain.

February 13

The Patience of Rain

If I were less resistant, rainy days would instruct me
in the art of prayer. The rhythm on the roof keeps tapping;
its relentless pulse could call the strokes of willed attention.

But the lower self wants quick results – God served up to it
after a quick helicopter ride to the mountain top –
no slow anguish, no long climbs – instant illumination.

The servant I've become has not yet the patience of rain,
but I'm strong enough to make this effort now: be, hold, now;
then regathering, coming back firmly to prayer: now, be.

February 14

Good Masters

Good masters allow that citizens be granted visits
to the palace. They must prepare and groom themselves, put on
cleanest garments, walk the miles carefully in gratitude
and hold themselves without collapsing into talk or tears.

One hour's visit can make the meaning of a man's whole life.
Saints have shaped themselves from the memory of one visit.
How lucky are we whose masters invite us frequently
and have even given us our own coded call to use
when we long to be gazing up at the great balcony.

February 15

Cutting the String

It's a day for breaking momentum, for cutting the string
of gains the lower self has made, for preventing habit
from forming in the spine. Here the right use of privation.
Take no food. Offer no opinion. Hatch no idea
of success. Postpone decisions. Entertain nobody.
Provide no water that the weeds can find. Promise nothing.
You will have enough to do ignoring the burning itch
of Satan's annoyance. Don't worry about wasting time.
(Time lets the universe run down.) Turn against the current,
face upstream, and stand still. Establish the heart of your will.

February 16

Swine

To imagine you can teach swine sufficient refinement
to appreciate pearls is vanity. Let swine be swine:
only then can their swininess be loved, their whininess
be heard as strange music. They (and you) are made to purpose,
and that they simply don't care about beauty is no worse
than the ignorance we don't think we're laboring under.

Lead the poor pig patiently to its right place at dinner.
You don't have to push it from behind, your eyes looking down.
What must happen to it is likewise happening to us.
Bring it gratefully to the celebration and taste, taste.

February 17

Gone

A mustache and dark glasses won't hide you; even a wig
won't do it. You really have to become invisible,
and to truly vanish, you must quit wanting attention,
much less applause, from everyone else you're imprisoned with.

Your desire to control how they regard you is your cell's
strong lock. Let it go and use the file of reason to cut
through your sense of obligation to imagination.
See, the way is clear. You can walk out of here and go home.

I know, you want to know exactly how one disappears.
It's simple. No one can see you remembering yourself –
no one but God and the Angels, that is, and they won't tell.
So come out from behind the veil of forgetting. Be gone.

February 18

The Objections

Remember, the lower self has a varied arsenal.
It's noisier rumblings – hunger, annoying discomforts,
squabbles with the words or the rude tone directed at it –
these are easy insurrections to raise the sword against.

More troubling are its cries for justice and freedom of choice,
which if examined unsentimentally amount to
Mr. Gut's pathetic plea for equality with God
and the right to live in imagination unto death.

Even more insidious are his alarms that the soul
threatens the health of the body, which needs more food, more rest,
less stress, less irritation. In the present, the body
rightly ruled rejoices to be the Eye's strained scaffolding.

You must know yourself, lest the earthsuit masquerade as real,
as truly you. The soul must distinguish what it is not
and train the steward in its holy discernment – the path
of renunciation, mindfulness that will not be fooled.

February 19

Nature

The large rabbit that visits my property each morning
brazenly uses the paved road as if it paid taxes.
The deer the same, stopping to arrogantly nose and taste
whatever is appealing. Even the cutest creatures
will take what they know they can get away with. They're not fools,
and they're not naïve. Underestimating animal
intelligence can be the ruin of a perfect garden.

Shooting the buggers doesn't solve the problem. We need them,
believe it or not: a few little spiders keep the house
free of much worse. Besides, nature is relentless; its will
puts ours to shame. We must give it its due, offer a place
and time for it to eat and drink and mate and defecate.
In truth, we are the guests, nature the host. We depend on
its brute hospitality to have a Guest of our own.

February 20

Nothing Better

There isn't anything better than this. Don't dismiss it.
Stay here and hold it. It's all you've got. The restless voices
and urges driving your search cannot recognize the truth
when it is right here in front of them, as it always is.

You create time by moving through space, by running away
from the present, which is not of time and which can be known
only by that part of you not of time. That part of you
is you, the soul. The rest – what you call yourself – is just flesh
branded with a name, moving through space, abuzz with a cloud
of thoughts that keep your awareness from knowing the present.

There isn't anything better than this. The awareness
of your attention now is all there really is. Stay here.
Don't run away. Don't flee into the cloud of forgetting.
In there your thoughts are flies stinging what cannot know itself.

February 21

Windless

These days I can come to know the slow erosion of life.
Paddling in place, getting no closer to the other shore,
I understand death as the only end to body's aches.
Neither terror nor encouragement comes from this knowledge.

I want to die opening like a lotus, kiss the sun
with my annihilation, but God wants me here, paddling,
bailing out these thoughts for you to study. What can you learn
from my life marooned in front of you, full of unborn love,
and to all your doubts and praise utterly untouchable?

February 22

Reduced

Sometimes the gelatin that holds my mélange of a life
together in its bruised imitation of unity
melts in the heat of events, and the "I" I try to be
for others and even for myself rudely falls apart.

It's panicky and humiliating but not all bad.
A more real "I" is left standing in the debris field, stumped
like a child who doesn't understand the question or know
who's asking. He just remains there being simply himself.

After all the you're-not-who-we-thought's in the head subside,
being reduced to a puzzled child is liberating,
and after a few such meltdowns, that child, that pure essence
can become aware of himself: then everything changes.

The "I" that was an assemblage of lies and ambitions
gives way to the "I" whose purity doesn't even need
to name itself, being innocently aware of all
the mind boundaries that keep everything from just being.

February 23

The Love Beyond Prayer

If silly, personal, petitioning prayer had power,
I would drop to my knees and gush forth the following cry:
Overwatching Angels, whose love and mercy operate
on a scale we can barely fathom, please loosen the bolts
on this pressure box of my life. I can't pull in a breath,
and my mind is swarmed with airless thoughts. Whatever I think
I am is imploding, and I feel useless in the world.

What's the problem with this prayer? First, the Angels don't want us
on our knees. They want us standing, spine stretched, eyes to Heaven.
Second, what we think we are must implode, shrivel and drop
so the invisibly bright souls we truly are can rise.
The pressure box metaphor is apt. The process is clear.
I think this prayer gets what's going on, what Angels must do.
So just how much do I want to learn the love beyond prayer?

February 24

Come Away

Turn off the television, push away from the table,
close your ears to the talk of swinish commerce, pinch your nose
as you step delicately around the rotting garbage.
The force-fed malnourishment of the mind and the senses
must end. You must be completely cleaned, replanted, watered --
parched no more in imagination's unslakeable thirst.

February 25

Cleaning Out

I should have abandoned them earlier, mercilessly
cutting off their sighs and pleadings, their cries and arguments.
There was nothing to be gained from studying their reasons
and connections, their families, their histories and hopes.
One can only enter Heaven with one's back turned to them,
moving away as they whimper and coo and snarl and curse.
They will starve without my attention, choke on my absence,
these parasites, self-loving voices who cannot know God.

February 26

The Mail

Who am I to be impatient that the mail isn't here?
Better to sit and watch my fingers as all by themselves
they tie and untie the laces on my old walking shoes.
I remember teaching them this trick when I was a boy,
and they've used it dutifully in service for decades.
The trick I was taught by Heaven is equally simple,
but I forget and wander off and the job goes undone,
like undelivered mail. Thank you, Angels, for your patience.

February 27

The Real Story

The lower self's narrative, imagination, is not
a succession of events disclosed with cogent comment;
rather it is a thing doubling back on itself, spasmed,
convoluted, a knot in the neck strangling higher mind,
coughing gibberish in love with itself, a thing to cut.
One's real life – the interruptions in this idiot's tale –
must be held breath to breath, humble being gasping for God.

February 28

Thirty Birds

It is true. Each of the thirty birds penetrates the cloud
with its perfect note. You do not remember all their names
in order yet, but you're practicing and will acquire them.
Each time you lift one on your finger and bid it sing forth,
a clear sky breaks and the light of the sun warms your forehead.
So simple the gift of this flock no man could think of it.

February 29

Not Today

What can be mined from today? It is an honest question,
but the language bears the trace of the devil's sleight of hand.
'Today' might as well be an aeon. The void's vastness lures
one away into fanciful thought. Rather be mindful
of this breath coming in to work. Mine the rich vein of now.

§

March 1

Guarding the Ascent

Between the great refinery and the sacred children
stands the ladder. Nectar made at the bottom must carried
to the top, so the children can mature and know themselves.
At the ladder's either end sit the dark one's defenses,
narrowings of the way where maraud the mindless thousands
who prey like ants on the climbing, nectar-bearing pilgrims.

So this is your job, my son: the poor pilgrims must get through.
In their great ascent, the nectar is transformed to honey –
the children's only food. You will be their sole guarantor.
See the moon. There are only two outcomes to its passage.

March 2

Allegory of a Lost State

An august guard-goose, proud in its prominence, at the gate
formidably stood. "What is your business?" it asked me.
"I'm delivering peace to the princess," I said meekly.
He bid me pass to do my job. The princess welcomed me
then sent me back with gratitude for the goose at the gate.
But alas, the goose had found another bird to instruct,
a beautiful broad-breasted brown hen. The two had wandered
in their talk, and the open path was filled with loud traffic
coming brutally on. This is all I can remember.
Where am I? Where have I put the princess's gratitude?

March 3

Together in a Storm

The noisy squall outside does not mean nature is averse.
We need a little resistance – swimming up a rapid –
to make our coming together meaningful. Unity
is a lost friend we must labor to bring home. Once inside
the upper room, quickened by each other, we toast to love
and understand God's little jest of he and she and me,
and the rough, belly-laughing winds outside we see to be
in on the joke in their own crude way. Do not demean them.

March 4

Call the Roll

The opposite of presence is absence. Isn't it odd
that a whole roomful of people can be not here, rather,
here and not be? What's also amazing is what happens
on the not being level: breakfast, lunch, dinner, careers,
births, deaths, wars, migrations, the rise and fall of…everything –
the tense, crowded hologram between nothingness and God.
So call the roll. Is anyone here today? School goes on.
Ah, so few here learning to be God, who alone is great.

March 5

Worship

Do not worship. Worship is the harlot's trick, spiriting
you off in potent feeling. Renounce it. Save your money.
It's not that much further to the portal in the temple.
Remember where the key is hidden. Choose the best handle.
Enter and begin your procession. When the harlot cries,
keep your back to her and move on. Your mind exists to keep
your will intact. At the last step when the priestess appears,
a weak will fails and you melt away, a dead worshipper,
but a firm mind will keep you there as you are escorted
in to learn the hospitality of the sacred ones.

March 6

Don't Believe Her

The prayer whore squats outside the garden. She will grab your knees
and pull you down. Her kind of beauty is ugly. Don't stop.
Would you die in the arms of the harlot's rank believing?
Listen! Your mind is circling for you. Answer, "Here I am."

March 7

If It Be Now

I'm ready now. I have prepared. Please do what you must do.
Now is the time to forsake all beliefs, all thoughts, all spurs
which kept the heart laboring on and the mind returning.
All that I was and have been falls away, abandoned clothes.
Now I'll see what is lost and what gained in departing here.
Only this I pray: do not let me swoon or faint away
at the terror or the majesty or the nothingness.
I want all the truth of God. Let my readiness be real.

March 8

Purgatory

Hell is the lack of awareness of God. I'm not joking
or playing with words: in the absence of the awareness
of God, the lower self rules a time-bound, comfort-based life.

Characterized by mindless obedience, residents
of hell work hard for a living and love their families.
They consume what they're taught to want, die mechanically
and fertilize the moon. More hopeful is purgatory
where one's awareness of God is dim, unsustained, too weak
to challenge the lower self when it demands and snatches.
One experiences oneself helpless, chewed, unable
to cry out, and worse, unable to die, yet God is here.

Reaching an understanding of God, we should not be shocked
to find ourselves in purgatory. We're not moon manure.
Awareness of God defines us: light trapped in tortured food.

March 9

Still Here

Can the lower self be executed or locked in jail
to starve? I'm afraid not. He owns the earthsuit you're leasing,
little soul, and if he dies, the suit will be repossessed.
You're unfinished and can't live on earth without an earthsuit,
so you must render to Mr. Gut his proper tribute.

However that does not mean that you forget your lineage.
Requiring his earthsuit does not mean you're starving in jail;
that he is lurking everywhere does not mean you're not here.
In fact, if he takes your suit and slips away in darkness,
or the whole earth dissolves including your feet, you're still here.

March 10

Produce

"Produce!" – the heart's relentless answer to every question.
"Produce!" – the shout that cuts short every thought. I make poems
from presence and presence from poems, my pen responding
to the steward's commanding pulse. In this work I'm of use
to the Angels: our little scull moves against the current,
back up from plain to foothill, to mountain snow, to pure air,
to unresisting blue, unconsolidated being.
This ascent to nothing defines each scale of time, each world,
age, lifetime, orbit, season, day, hour, breath producing now.

March 11

Having Time

Do you have time? How lucky you are! Whenever I think
I have time – enough time to really accomplish something –
a trickle of interruptions grows into a cascade
of sudden necessities and the time I thought I had
evaporates and I'm late planning tomorrow's schedule.

It's like I'm tied down to an anthill of details and lose
sting by sting all sense of scale. Why can't I just surrender
to the present, be its humble unrestricted captive,
and let time's caravan travel on? It doesn't need me.
But you, you have time. You've tied your camel to your own neck.

March 12

Tired?

The only thing that doesn't lead to trouble later on
is being present. Karma simplified. If you are not
present, you're trapped in thought, locked inside the racquetball court,
playing with the devil, who looks remarkably like you.
No matter how hard or how delicately you hit it,
the damned ball keeps bouncing off the walls at you forever.
How long will it take you to get tired of it? Nine lifetimes?
The key is here in this poem that by now you must know
you're reading. As you are the door, don't knock. Open yourself.

March 13

Prayer Rug

You can't think your way out. The best thinking that can be done
deduces that you cannot lift the rug you're standing on.
All the mental churning, all the effect analysis
still leaves you "you," and to become more conscious, precisely
that "you" must depart. How to begin? Total surrender.

Remembering God is not thinking. Remembering God
is submission to a state. The only thing left for you –
a completely new you – is to keep all the objections
from the old you at bay – a silent, selfless constancy.
Now the prayer rug rises by itself, a magic carpet.

March 14

Breathing

If you know your breathing, you can begin to know the rest.
Riding the rhythm of breath, your awareness can direct
the opening of all the seas and all the little coves
of being: the tempests below; the blessing, sunlit heart;
the high silken streams where silent swans move without motion
through the narrow straight to rest before the Eye whose seeing
is the finest prayer. All can be, if you know your breathing.

March 15

Transports

If Angels did not sometimes kiss our foreheads and bring forth
our souls for an extended sunning, this work would in weeks
wither and crumble to chalky obedience, dead form.
So strong our feelings, so believable our inner talk,
our power to renounce them quietly loses light; the heart
tires and forgets to fight. To seek sustainedly the state
of God requires Angel transport, gifted minutes aloft
reminding us in surprised delight what we are and aren't.

March 16

Privacy

The work of the body is to host its secretive Guest.
Silently here, the shy dear resides so unremembered
that one thinks one is alone in the house. (That's what thinking
mostly does – fortifies the illusion of privacy.)

When one at last discovers one has company, one lives
to serve or one seals the knowledge away in any one
of a thousand closets of forgetting. (That private self
is stubborn and has the powerful claim of possession.)

A servant must arise from one's better nature to take
command of the property, put it in pleasing order,
purify it so the Guest feels welcome. (Helping the soul
to be surpasses anything one can do in private.)

March 17

Merely Everything

You get all of God's attention that you can be and hold
in this moment now, and the price is merely everything
you think, every urgency to move in body and mind.
So if you want God to acknowledge you, uplift your eyes
and be aware of yourself in the struggle to be still.
And don't expect a grand entrance. God is already here.

March 18

The Ledge

I cannot quite get my hand over the top of the cliff,
so I hang here between climbing and falling, protecting
a crumbling stability and groping for an angle
of ascent. Whatever happens, I am grateful to God
for all I have been given. Above me on the flat ground
crowning this precipice, a temple should be built holding
this height in view, securing the lifetimes of attention
it has taken to earn this place. What will extend my reach
these last inches? What new worthiness must my heart summon?

March 19

The Flood

We were but children when the levy ruptured and flooded
the fields far as we could see, drowning all simplicity
and shaping our pliant minds to an artificial sea.

Behind us and above, up the levy, on the river's
distant side stretch fields of abundant light, beckoning us
to remember, rise and cross. We were not always bounded
by an artificial ocean. We have a heritage
of light and endless skies rewarding flight. We can unlearn
the stranded life imagined here, remember and return.

Let us step back and turn our gaze up high, and take the step
that quickens breath till breathing is the echo of a life
arisen in the sky, unlimited and free to fly.

Spring --- Maturity

> *A name is only the guest of reality.*
>
> *Chuang Tzu*

> *Prayer is the rejection of concepts.*
>
> *Evagrios the Solitary*

March 20

In the Movie Theater

Once when I was twelve, I went to the movies to avoid
the fierce glare of July. The film was bad – British slapstick –
but they played it just for me: no one else bought a ticket.
I felt honored to be there alone in the theater.

The whole vast room chilled to a shiver, the darkness conquered
by the emptiness, I marveled at how innocently
stupid the movie was – moonlight and shadows on the wall
of this comforting cave. Later Plato would explain it.

I remember this episode as vividly as now:
darkness, vastness, emptiness, cold, amusing illusion –
and vanity honored to be alone in it. Angels
had projected as a lesson the image of the womb
my scared little self still inhabits, still won't abandon
for the hot, sunburned walk home in the all-dissolving light.

March 21

How Else?

This thought now forming – this one –will desert you. Don't trust it.
See, there it goes and already a new speaker on stage
trading wampum for your precious attention. You'll hear him,
but you mustn't believe him. Guard your heart with both hands crossed.
If you sit here, they'll keep coming. Stand up and walk. Leave them.
Your attention feeds this whole world. How else can it exist?

March 22

True Will

True will is the assertion of the soul, not mere desire.
It does not crave candy, curry promotion or chase sex.
True will engenders and sustains the highest attention –
the awareness of attention – and while it is concerned
that the earthsuit cooperate, it promises nothing.

When the body obeys – submits to will in its breathing,
its alignments, its activities, and its character –
contented states result, little oases of delight
in the windy desert of life in time. So don't worry
about the body's wants: just be the soul aware of them.

If your will is mature and holds on, eventually
the body will capitulate to it, as it were choose
awareness over wanting, and settle in contentment:
the earthsuit will consent to be worn as a horse submits
at last to a benevolent rider in no hurry.

March 23

The Thing Time Can't Chew On

Why be concerned that the car is breaking down? Think it through.
At some point, it will be a non-car, melted and alloyed
and reformed into wheelbarrows or flatware. Let it go.
Your body is no different. Sooner than you believe,
some child will be swinging on the branch which is now your arm;
a monkey will use what was your skull to capture termites.
Look to the thing that does not change, the thing time can't chew on.

Locate it. Here it is – the thing that doesn't forget you
as you're reading this, the thing that watches your mind reading.
Be concerned about this. Be this thing, this state. Don't let go.
Don't be lured away by change, death, lucky breaks, strange noises.
Let the world fashioned by your senses swim beneath the Eye.

March 24

Your Own Pedaling

Take off the trainer wheels. Quit quoting Krishna and Plato
and Jesus and see if your own legs have sufficient thrust
to hold you up and keep you balanced. Stretch your movements past
their borders into shocking certainty. See if your mind
can hold its aim no matter what pretty things go rushing
past you on the road of distraction. What authority
do your own words assert on the souls of your companions?

It's proper to be reverent to the Angels, pious
and solemn before their works, but your own artistry must
seek to penetrate the bright realm to which they summon you.
High respect is not enough. You can't emulate your way
into Heaven. Plato won't do your pedaling for you.

March 25

Sneaking Out

I know you -- you, glimpsing through the curtain of time. Hold still.
Look at me. Let our eyes meet. I'll follow you out of here
if you point the way. All the poor souls in this theater
are so rapt in the play, they will not see me leave my seat,
slip backstage, catch your quickening gleam and quit the building.

For as long as my fuel lasts – I've been saving – let's tour
eternity. I promise to share everything you've taught
when your breeze delivers me back, though you and I both know
these clappers will receive my tale as a dutiful boy
receives his grandma's kisses. But so what, I'm coming up.

March 26

The Whole in the Head

There's a whole in the crown of my head. I must locate it
precisely. I know it's here, but it's covered up with thoughts
and matted with belief and fear. The mind doesn't want it
opened, or the prisoner God will escape, and the whole
beautiful universe will dance and sing God's sweet return.
What a disaster for the mind, for thought, belief and fear.

March 27

It Doesn't Matter

It doesn't matter that your name is not known to the world.
It doesn't matter that you have sinned or that you will sin.
It doesn't matter that God for you is blank, unfathomed
and that you find praying to be just talking to yourself.
It doesn't matter that you often want to take your gold
and head south to the sunshine and sit by the pool and drink
yourself blind and deaf to all painful opportunities.

What matters is that these words are in your ears now, and now
you are aware of them migrating to your brain, and now
you know yourself in a separate way, and this instant
your heart turns and agrees to listen to your silent prayers.

March 28

Tool

My body is being aged over, disconcertingly
so to the lower self; movement is restricted and sex
put in dusty storage. But it's not all troubling. My throat
no longer clings to words. It surrenders at the first sign
of their unnecessity. My eyes have relaxed, gently
dropping their focus down and in to the tip of my nose.
The brow and crown can breathe now, and now is just what they breathe,
waiting out of time for the next message they will forward
to the right hand ready with its pen. What a well made tool!

March 29

Why Now?

My stocks are crumbling, my retirement postponed, my life ruined –
so why does my heart want me here in the poetry chair?
It's simple. It doesn't matter what sets the hummingbird's
wings a fluttering – honeyed flower or fatal alarm –
the energy is there, the God wavelength. Prolonged presence
is possible now. Events are stirring. So here I sit
together with all those outside of time who can't retire.

March 30

Melancholy

In my tiny cosmos, the feeling of abandonment
has a wide orbit and visits rarely, but when it comes,
its effect is profound. The shadows deepen, the bridges
between thought and desire close down. The great destination
offers no light. What to do? Savor the melancholy.

This darkling condition, the space created by divorce,
is not hell. Having to make one's own light under a cloud
for a few hours – or days – is not damnation. God remains
available, but the ecstasy one associates
with God shows her roots and wrinkles and can't keep the party
going by getting drunk and taking off her clothes to pose.

March 31

No Problem

Some problems are not to be solved or fixed; the reminders
of mortality, the signs of shrinking time – some dear stings,
and lucky lapses – are to be cherished, not corrected.
So palpable the illusion of living in the world,
it's said sometimes the dead don't know they're dead. So when a stab
of pain surprises me, or I find myself gone cold blank
on the name of the person I'm talking to, I'm restored
to God's humility, the presence wearing my exile
in this earthsuit on this planet. Much better. No problem.

§

April 1

If You Can

If you can, believe nothing, and let that knowless nothing,
hanging there beyond belief, be. Carry it to the bath.
Let the steam unwrinkle it till it's so perfectly smooth
the air can't cling to it; then take nothing from the hanger,
and in no motion put it on and disappear from mind.

April 2

Dazzled

Something dazzling may be harder to use than something dire.
Beauty and pleasure satisfy so much of us that God
gets cut out of the deal, but painful things, threatening things
have us calling to God to come sit high at our table.

Truthfully, we are God – you and I –except when we're not.
We forget and become dazzled with touch and taste; we think
we are thinking, but our thinking is in thrall to pleasure
which in turn needs the imagined protection of power
and wealth, and too soon we've forgotten that we've forgotten.

Luckily we can still die; most luckily we can die
before we die, remembering that what we truly are
does not die, but would turn to God and face God and be God
and let dazzled, pleasured, painful, dire things be what they are.

April 3

Forward to Zero

From his rigid coma, Atlas holds the world up to you,
and all the mindfulness that it produces as it spins
amounts to a few fireflies in vast night. And I who know
the secret of secrets have spent my life forgetting it.

Forgive me, Angels, my complicity in what the world
has made of me. Forgive me wasting so much of my time.
Forgive me for listening to the serpent, for dreaming
in the sleep of his whisper, for wanting to be a name.
Forgive these thoughts, this prayer, this substitute remembering.

April 4

Together

Is this little poem born in presence or in the black
closet of imagination? Where is my attention
as my pen moves along leaving these words behind for you?
By what light are you reading? Are we together in God?

April 5

Politely

I am the interruptions in the earthsuit's inner talk,
the moments when the hanging man feels the taut rope of death
and the stupid smile slackens, and the eyes know what they see.
How does the devil lure me back when I have departed
for a real moment, holding the rope by my own poor strength?
He asks how I got here, and I politely start to think.

April 6

Say It

All imagination is vanity – man's chief weakness,
and leaving imagination is like dying – being
ripped away by divine reason to which one has not yet
surrendered past all thought of mercy. (On a larger scale,
isn't dying merely being snatched out of this earthsuit
one imagines oneself to be and left a naked soul?)
So what sharp single-sound command can produce surrender
to the divine naked wisdom always here? Say it. Be.

April 7

Time and Language

"In the beginning was the Word," simply means that in time –
the dimension in which the soul struggles for its freedom,
the highest thing is the simplest and greatest syllable
of language. But as language grows elaborated, dense,
and pulls the soul down into airless thought, we must be wise.
Use language sparingly, one clear syllable at a time,
and mount the clear syllables to the highest one – the one
that in the beginning already is: Be. You've begun.

April 8

First One Allows

First one allows: this is the great suffering – not the pain
of resisting but the surrendering beyond instinct.
Let be – the world, the mind, the devil's dire grip on your throat,
let be all the wrong ideas, all the wasted effort
of the whole teeming herd of humanity. All attempts
to save anything or anyone must be abandoned
and everything, even the vanity of forgiveness,
must be forgiven. Then we too can be – the beginning.

April 9

Shove Off Then

I say that's enough. We can cast off now. No more waiting
for a friendlier sky. No more provisioning. The thoughts
of what we might need are endless; the ship already sits
so low in the water as to tax our will. Shove off then,
and row, row, row, on till the air warmed by the climbing sun
has found and filled our sails; and we can watch from the firm deck
the procession of the world our watching makes beautiful.

April 10

Reverence

How to reverence the Angels? Remembering their state
allows us to know. When one is at peace, one only wants
harmony, so all that is crude, roughhewn, loud, violent,
brutal, brusque, acerbic, noisome, full of force or snoring
is unwelcome. The work we do to protect our presence
is the same by which we respect the Angels. Be loving
to your own state, and Heaven will never be offended.

April 11

Open

If your throat were an open gate, the heart's praises of God
could pass through and light your brain, but it is too often stuck,
and the praises, which know only the present, cannot wait,
deteriorate, and dribble into conversation,
and there you are, talking to yourself inside your head, dead.

April 12

Poet

Yes, child, you are a poet, a species not quite prophet,
but what kind of poetry will you write? There are but these:
one, the poetry of God; two, the poetry of death.
As poetry is praise, you may praise God or you'll praise death.
Praising God has a long apprenticeship, but praising death
gives you immediate access and great variety.
Just look at all the dying things. What fine freedom of choice!
God made you a poet to sing your own songs up or down
creation. All songs end in silence, all poets eaten.
What would you be consumed by as you sing
    your songs of praise?

April 13

Worry

So it did not kill me, for here I am. The worrying
proved to be the worst part of it. Why don't I understand?
Why can't I learn this lesson? I'm alive to bring God here,
and when God has fulfilled that visit, I'll be gone – no me
without God, but who'd want to be anywhere without God?
So all this worry – about death, taxes, bad performance,
looking like an idiot, being kicked out of the club –
all this worry has nothing to do with the love of God.
Where then does it come from? Find out and you'll find the devil.
Worries are the devil's whispers, and we leave God's mansion
to listen to them. We leave God to wander and worry.

April 14

Perfect Words

Perfect your hospitality to get the Guest to come.
Delighted with the food – the gate silently protected –
she reveals secrets as she walks with you in the garden.
There is no greater source of the flowering truth we crave.
Unless she visits, even the best sprouts will feed the ants.
So get the house ready. Clear the entry. Use your best hand
on the invitation. No faux pas. Find the perfect words.

April 15

The Difference

The devil responds to irritation, but he does so
to protect his world. Danger, discomfort, loss of status,
boredom, betrayal – against these from his filthy bunker
he orders out his troops. But in God there is no danger,
no loss or waste of time, no suffering not offering
love an opportunity. The devil is a devil
because of what he's made of – mortality and hatred
of mortality. You are you because the mortal prince
in your heart, God's outpost, dies reminding you who you are.

April 16

Gratitude

Be grateful for your gratitude: it is you who needs it.
Gratitude waters the heart and makes it fertile for prayer;
prayer is the attention in which the steward knows itself
and acts and so matures. Angels can use our gratitude,
but they don't need it. It makes their job a bit easier:
it softens the shells of the nuts they must crack – the humans
in which we're growing. So don't think I'm slighting gratitude.
Warm tears or not, the Angels' love is sweet to acknowledge.

April 17

Travel

Travel is travail, but one can't live without traveling.
The passage to a new city is choked, like being pulled
through a snake, but once you're there, you'll have a plate of delights
put before you, replenished each breath till your money's gone.
Now money's always going; just make sure that memories
are forming at equal rate. And travel makes memories
because it rewards your best attention more distinctly.
The best travel? From wherever you are to the present,
and while you remain here, be mindful of the city's shrine.

April 18

Circulation

Let's be practical about this: You can't do it alone.
If your love doesn't circulate, it pools, consolidates,
grows fetid and rank. The Eye turns up its nose, so to speak;
your limp discipline huffs on behind an unbreathing mask.

You must give your love to people, to the human beings
above and below who reach for you. Don't whine about waste.
You don't have to kiss everybody at the shopping mall,
but a treasured few to honor and protect you must have.

So much the better, so much the more profound and cherished
is your love if it flows among those chosen by Angels
to be your lovers. To them the fumbled words, the unhealed
scars of awkwardness, the misunderstandings don't matter.

Then you can simply love, share delight, sip the wine of truth
while the flames in your hearts touch and kiss. O sweet abundance!
But even mislaid in a ward of comatose people,
be practical: let a silent current flow from your heart.

April 19

On Guard

Let them hate me if they need to hate. Better me than God.
God marvels at hate but is not curious about it.
God will not be interrupted to study what will not
be transformed; rather God places me at the gate, steadfast
and grateful to be employed, and I turn the haters back
down the road to the snaky cavern to share self-pity
and plot among themselves their next assault. Thus earth troubles
Heaven, but God is not disturbed because I stand watchful,
minding and guarding the gate, tasting the heart of each thought.

April 20

I'm Back Now

Ah, I remember now! I had been attending to God,
enough to rise just a bit, enough to melt the edges
of self-importance. The lower self was getting bothered –
crossed arms, clenched throat, thoughts of what the kitchen had to offer –
when that sultry girl sauntered on stage and removed her clothes,
and I turned to watch, forsaking God for yet another
naked girl in my head: the lower self pimps his daughters.
This sad desertion took only seconds, but I'm back now,
disturbed that I would leave my post, amazed God
  brought me back.

April 21

Needing No Task

I do not want to waste this time, this time, though there's nothing
I want to do. Why clean? The dust defiantly returns.
Why climb to clear the gutters for a storm merely presumed?
Why read when there's already too much in my crowded brain?
My wrinkled earthsuit prefers to sit piled in just this chair.

But even in this fit of nonexertion I can be.
My soul is not asleep. It hovers contentedly here,
sustaining itself aloft in presence, needing no task
but its own being. If nothing's getting done, yet the day
is not wasted. This stillness nurtures what I truly am.

April 22

To Own

Losses hurt. Even an inexpensive token – the scarf
my dear son gave me – leaves a raw spot where it had nestled
and attached, and bigger losses completely capsize one
and keep breaking up with sudden disorienting doubt
the reason, the coherence, the next step, the coming breath.

To own is to depend. The stark face off in each moment
between the now and what I no longer have confuses
what is left of me. I have lost you. Were we ever real?
The brutal, unleashed present leaps right for my naked throat
and leaves not a word to protest, not a thought to lie with.

April 23

Remorse

O God, these attacks of cold remorse for a life wasted
are so deep and believable. This is the lower self's
nuclear weapon, vaporizing all value and worth.
Coming out of this cloud, separating, finding a perch
of pure observation, one sees only a dead landscape
and breathes meaningless air. Even your love kindles no joy.

This is the bottom of hell, below any cognizance
of justice, any meaning of suffering, any sense.
This is the depth to which the lower self will go to hold
the soul in time, and the soul's only response is to watch
in unbelieving, accepting the nothing of nothing
till the hard, clear truth has liberated the eternal.

April 24

Take Me

I am so tired that I cannot manufacture meaning
from duties I do to keep my body fed and sheltered.
If my will were stronger, I'd be a beggar in the world.

I would be no one, namelessly absorbed in you, O God.
Let the current of your being dissolve the ruined borders
of my separateness. Take me. I am too weak to die.

April 25

Not Yet

With ease the lower self turns mastery to mockery,
laughing at the forms the steward needs to do its duty.
Though it will never breathe the formless truth, the lower self
well understands the ultimate futility of form.

There is a time for such insight: when the form has grown fat,
torpid, merely traditional, and efforts made through it
obediently unproductive; but that time is not
the lower self's to say. The Angels know when something's dead.

When it is time to let the feathers fall and naked go
and be invisible to eyes requiring form to see,
an Angel, not your ridiculing fellow prisoner,
will inform you and lead you awestruck from the useless cell.

April 26

Wet

Five straight days of rain makes one dumb and sofa-dog lazy.
The water slowly erases ambition and slackens
the nerve lines. The staccato parade of drops on gutters
is the only thing keeping mindfulness from leaving town.

With bare work it becomes anticlimactically clear
that all but God is illusion. Be careful. In this state
sleep can come to you as a quiet, listless concession,
a permission to devalue wet days of nonevent.

April 27

Father and Son

The son is the hero of the father, and the father
learns time from the son until he can no longer visit
the son's earth save in patience and mercy. Open that gate
and Heaven and earth communicate, and father and son
are one, absolving in compassion's arc all mortal birth.

April 28

Dog

A house dog is a love sponge, there to soak up affection
we have no other place to put – we have so much of it.
The transitory tenderness of just two people floods
the floors and dries to a sticky, lint-catching residue
that makes movement halting and unnatural. Unexpressed
love attracts thoughts and becomes dangerous. Bring in the dog.

Here, pretty doggy. My heart is baking a little treat
just now, and spilling out from the oven onto the floor
it must come. O thank you God – I mean dog – for cleaning up
this mess of extra love my heart can't stop making: my life.

April 29

Hors D'Oeuvre

Don't read this wolfishly or dismissively. It is here
to be tasted, savored, digested, absorbed by the blood,
delivered to the heart and slowly, completely burned up
opening the passage to the Eye and the Crown and out
to the great torrent flowing down from where you must return.

This verse is an hors d'oeuvre to awaken a hunger,
a longing for God's attention. It can stop your descent
for just a few heartbeats, urge the complete turn you must make,
intimate the miracle behind and above your mind.

April 30

Asked to Leave

The ringing in my ears used to be annoying – no more.
As it grew constant, much like the current of the cosmos,
I became the annoyance and troubled myself so much
that finally I was asked to leave. Now the universe
rings steady, aware of its own keen, untroubled hearing.

§

May 1

Mine

Bring them on, Mr. Gut! Let loose from hell all your monsters.
I can withstand them, and my claim is not rashly spoken.
Let them swim up from the cold-bellied bottom of being
to flash their bloodstained teeth, their sickening yellow eyeballs.
Let their gory drool smear my floor, and their putrid odor
gag my open throat. I am ready for their piercing screams,
their talons, their ambush waiting round each darkened corner.

The tingling fear, the shallowed breath, the razors at the edge
of touch – all your symptoms and signatures convince no more.
You are no longer master of my body, ancient brain.
It is mine now to align with Heaven, map its domains
and mine from its mortality an eternal jewel.

May 2

Earth and the Soul

If all the mad convulsions, the churn of melting matter –
yes, even human stuff – that this stomach of an earth makes
of itself could touch the soul, then Heaven would disappear
to the Eye. But earth is not Heaven, nor was meant to be.
The soul strengthens itself by affirming what it is not.
It is not matter breaking down, or conflict, tragedy,
horror, loss or dying. It sees and is not what it sees.
It knows itself best watching beauty and courage arise
and nobly fail, leaving vacancies of perfect silence.

May 3

At Last

It's time to get back to work and finish this small staircase.
I'm getting old, and it's too risky to jump when I want
to go in and enjoy the certainty of a real fire.
So let's return attention to the rhythm and the theme
of this little labor. When the final step is finished,
I'll stand square shouldered in the doorway silently breathing
the infinite possibilities of my vacant home.

May 4

Ransom

We descend into time to make appointments, to schedule
activities that keep the flesh maintained and the great lie
of "I" groomed and exercised, but we don't want to stay down
very long, not long enough to believe it anyway.
No, we want to climb back up, reclaim the great truth of Eye
and breathe it all the way home, disappearing into God.

We reincarnate every few seconds, do our brave work
and return. And what is that work? Why do we live this way?
To remind matter of God. To quicken it, to give it
a wink of remembering, a kiss to start a longing.
We ransom the return of the runaway universe.

May 5

Understood

One tries to tune one to the other, the mind to the heart,
restraining them, keeping them pure of all the lies the world,
which includes the instinct, promises in its constant woo.
"Who are you?" the incense asks at last. No, do not answer.
With one bite of the pronoun "I," you will be taken down.

Stay up there on your cross, friend, leaving it only to rise
further, for a few seconds out of time, into Godspace.
With your keen mind watching, your heart rooted in forgiveness,
you can let the world pass by transformed into what it is,
your love understood in the all and nothing that is God.

May 6

Worthiness

To trust Angels, you have to be close enough to feel them.
If they are an idea or a belief, you're too far.
The pilgrimage to visit them is one kind of effort,
but to actually get into the same room with them
requires that you be an Angel, not a poor supplicant.
Are you seeking help or favor? Stand out there in the court
of your worthiness. When you can be in here, you are here.

May 7

Poetry

It is easy to forget that the art of poetry
is not the aim of poetry. The art is a cluster
of techniques learned by a mind housed in a dancing body,
a body sensitive to rhythm whose heart cannot help
making music. Words are the notes and thought the passages.

The aim of poetry is to let elevated states
drop ladders to earth that readers may climb to seek those states.
You see, the state writes the poem. The poem drops to earth,
passing through the poet's mind, heart and body, a descent
into verse. The readers are trackers pursuing the scent
of the state, breathing it as they ascend above the words.

May 8

Cul-de-Sac

The human experience finds itself repeatedly
in the cul-de-sac of "I." It seems all roads lead to it.
Most people just build a house there and forget about it.
Soon the mail starts to come, and deliveries of all kinds
attest to the identity's steady residency.

But the address and the house and the cozy dead end street
do not a real I make, nor the reflexive reference
of names and language, nor the credible complications
of the body. Do not let the desire to know yourself
get stuck at the end of the street of "I." You are not that.

May 9

Like Nothing

What will it be like when I am one with God? Like nothing.
Language will not contain it. Similes can't stretch that far.
Just stay on the road – breathing, walking, loving the presence
that is more and more the closer one gets. The Bridge of Death
keeps the road going across the Gorge of No Ideas.
I'll dump my name over the side and proceed, more and more
here, even as now, more and more not anything but God.

May 10

Coffee House

I once wrote a verse play in a place like this, a few lines,
perhaps a stanza or a speech, each day for many weeks.
I was drinking strong coffee then, enough to kill me now.
Age is enlightening and mellowing, good in most ways
except the increasing decrepitude, wisdom's great price.

The verse play sits in a notebook, and I sit here writing
this verse you're reading, the present having swallowed the past,
the future in disabled imagination, unreal.
Here we are, two poems of now, perched above time, watching
our plays move through their carefully written entanglements.

May 11

Loss

Pain clings both to real loss and to lost opportunity.
One leaves a hole over which the flesh may never reknit;
the other's pale beauty in the clouds mocks what you have not.
From both the mind is urgent to flee, desperate to heal,
but the mind's driven thoughts can't evade what the heart must feel.

Entrust your heart to the vacancy, the sense of never
being whole again; rather be what you are and feel it.
Let the heart clean the room; let the echoing ache resound
from deep within forever. Be true to its dry, hollow
welcome; God's shameless, humble being seeks just such shelters.

May 12

The Way Back

Thoughts are not evanescent fireflies gone in a moment.
They could be, but the whole body clings to them, worships them
like stars, lacquers them over with hope, pride and heroism.
The result is a false self supreme within its capsule,
its membrane of calcified thought. A few years into life,
that shell is all one knows. Reality is forgotten,
and the only way back to it and to the creator
is through a shattering seismic surrender that lets go
of all thought and welcomes the terror of devouring God.

May 13

My Thinking

There's one sure way to know that my thinking is in error:
it feels like my own, unaccompanied by God's presence.
In the awareness of God, the heart radiates patient
love and compassion, and my thinking is a poor function
willing to serve as it can but always in deference
to the heart's far-sighted intelligence. God governs all.

When I ignore God's presence, my thinking sits expertly
in the sedan chair of righteous logic and is carried
by the slaves of vanity in a parade concluding
aptly at the shrine of our first bipedal ancestor.
If I suddenly glimpse God in the crowd, I pay no mind,
resolute in my fabricated duty to us all.

Why would I prefer my own thinking over God's presence?
The mechanical universe expands, its back to God,
rushing and screaming outward till exhausted – nullity.
My functions are carried on those rapids. To swim upstream,
to turn and find God above the current, is to deny
the grip of matter, the esteem of men, the common death.

May 14

Psalm

Having murdered, David was given no rest from the sword.
True, he made such great poetry from his exile from peace
that Christ sang a verse as his own sacrifice perfected.
But David's breathtaking temple stalled on the battlefield.

Late in life, Solomon offered space for alien gods
in exchange for sexual license, and the kingdom split.
The transgressions of great men are sewn in a pavilion
of suffering, and all who witness there must share the cost.

Such is the economy of awakening: we learn
forgiveness of our enemies, our teachers and ourselves.
When it is absolute, when we blame no one, we are free,
and can with a long breath intone the psalm and take our leave.

May 15

Empty Church

Herded by the guide, the little procession of pilgrims
enters the church where each in singular reverence lights
a small, sturdy candle at the back of the vaulted room
and moves off to hushed prayer. Through it all the guide's attention
keeps everything ordered, resolute, free from distraction
till a strange but firm prompting in the very air and space
informs him that his time is up and that he will become
a disturbance if he stays, not allowing the great church,
empty and illuminated, to breathe, to be itself.

May 16

The Secret of Your Transports

You cannot give anything to anyone who is not
seeking it. It is natural to want to share the first
florescences of God, to present yourself overbrimmed
with new love, but to one not longing for liberation
from forces he has bravely faced and sincerely studied,
your enthusiasm is an idiot's energy
to be politely borne. You must be still, hold the secret
of your transports tenderly. There is a widening gorge
between the world and you, and you are only visible
to those already yearning and trying to reach across.

May 17

Pause

The first response, quicker than thought and firmer than feeling,
follows from training or the lack of it. If the latter,
it will arise from the most mechanical elements,
be as automatic as the fall of something severed;
while the former marks valuation hardened to habit.

But neither saving the child from the flames nor retreating
to a safe distance involves the soul. The observing soul
engenders action by putting a stay on reaction,
by consciously prompting the pause that permits compassion,
by stopping time to let the wise, consoling heart catch up.

May 18

Pertaining

"It does not pertain to me," is the lower self's best lie.
Look at the sky – already you have moved closer to God;
but the lower self scolds, "Yes, there's the sky. It's fine. So what?"
And it revs its thought cycle to roaring and speeds away
with you on the back, holding on breathless, scared to let go.

Does death pertain to you? See that deep ditch beside this road,
more like a gorge? It just goes down and down and out and out,
and the road ahead is starting to tilt toward it. You must
make a chain of remembering, a bright sequence of links
tied to the silent self that doesn't live in gravity.

Does God pertain to you? Remember, God's concern extends
only to the actual, not the imaginary,
so if God does not pertain to you, you may disappear
with the next thought. Better question: Do you pertain to God?
And just how? Is God the sky? The gorge? Both? All? Everything?

May 19

Casting Off

This truth bears repeating: the tongue is the head of the snake,
the alimentary serpent, the whispering tempter.
It is impossible to enter imagination
when the tongue is soft, tranquilized: then the inner talk stops.

With the tongue relaxed and inactive, the heart's distillate
rises unresisted through the throat's narrow valve and waits
for the eyes to clear, to give themselves to what's before them.
Then efforts bear fruit, and the teaching touches miracles.
The Eye opens and the Crown levitates, and God is not
anything but everything, and you are nothing but God.

Clear the way for prayer. Find the charm that puts he snake to sleep,
so unimpeded tides of breath can flow from lowest spine
to highest head. Let the body lift to light, the arms rise.
Now you are ready to be, to climb, to cast off from time.

May 20

Imaginary

When you have verified that you are imaginary,
death loses its power. Now don't be silly about this:
The alimentary snake around which the body forms
is real at its level, and the body's needs when urgent
can dominate identity and override all else,
but you know that's not what I mean. Rather, I mean the swarm
of social pulsions and associations nervously
energized, bound, and collectively referenced as "I."

"I" forms itself from the refuse of social relations –
comparing, worrying, inner talking, striving to please.
The instinctive element is often pulling the strings,
but the puppet wouldn't move without believing it's real.
It isn't. It's imaginary. Fear and vanity.
When all that dies, when that whole accumulation scatters,
something will still be there. Don't name it, for in doing so
you sublet it to "I." Far better to simply let be.

May 21

Underwear

It can seem like a parlor trick, this "being present" thing,
like a successful back flip or a quick brain-tickling pun.
You get a taste of uberstate then everything resumes.
It's freaky, it's fun, but nothing to build a life around.
so your hamster mind drags your fooled heart back to the hell wheel.

In truth, being present is more like scratchy underwear,
always there between your name and earthsuit, unforgotten,
its friction slowly changing you, forcing your mind to be
still just to bear it, letting nothing unneeded move you.
Over time, decades, you breathe and perspire pure acceptance.

And here you are, your heart delighting in direct address
of God's own certainty, your life overbrimmed with being.

May 22

Humbled

How does one become more humble? The urge is to crush pride,
to put stones in one's shoes and walk stooped, to fast from delight.
Nope. You're still on stage, impressing the fan club in your head,
still wanting applause from refined folk you've conjured from clouds.
The puffy show will go on. Rather you must hide yourself,
become an empty seat in the theater, sneak backstage,
observe the machinery, find God behind the curtain.

Yes, it's true, God is invisible but can still be known
as the one aware of what you're seeing, the one humming
in your forehead, answering your breathing. God's awkward steps
will jostle you, but over time a dance from your embrace
will form and become all you care about. The gasps and sighs
from the crowd will still find your ears, but you will not wonder
for what joke they in this moment now have forgotten you.

May 23

Un

I took the dog to the vet today for vaccinations.
The doctor said, "These last three years, so they'll be her last ones."
Something undog in the dog conceded the doc's verdict,
but understanding death wasn't nearly as important
as the farmland she gazed at on our ride home or the treat
she eagerly accepted for her cooperation.

She's got it right. No ideas about death. Impressions
right here allow the truth to separate itself from mind.
The death sentence is a thing of words; the authority
of the speaker is irrelevant. When it arrives, death
will be impressions in the moment, an experience
of real being discovering what it is not and is.

May 24

Fast Donkey

It's true what the Teacher's been warning us about these days:
Between breaths, between syllables in a word, the donkey
can interject itself. That's one fast donkey. What on earth
could it want, this smartest and fastest of beasts? Everything,
of course, and especially not to be ridden. One thing
is in our favor. This earthbound marvel can only work
unwatched. Turn on the light, watch it determining your moves
and responses, and it flees. Did you giggle at the thought
of a donkey faster than sound? That was it, tickling you,
keeping your hands off the light switch lest you find the saddle.

May 25

Gusher

Sometimes a gusher of finer energies rushes past
the steward helpless in surprise. To be out of control
is shocking and embarrassing and dangerous and loud
and wondrous and ecstatic and astonishing and pure.
The flood might come forth as sticky sentiment, coarse movement,
or incessant talk, for which St. Paul apologizes.

If one is touched by witnessing the sudden abundance,
the Eye and the Crown can partake in the meal. More often
one is left bothered and sheepish and full of self-judgment.
Do not blush at the breakdown. Straighten your cap. The earth needs
volcanoes just as it needs vistas of husbanded farms.
The overflow done, lightly kiss the befuddled steward.

May 26

The Best Use of Time

An angry worm has slithered in between my heart and head.
It slipped past my exhausted watch, hid in my throat and spread
its poison up and down my breathing. My fevered thoughts twist,
and my hostage heart is clenched, pounding like a brutal fist.

What to do? Nothing. Trust no movement of the hands or feet.
Be patient. Wait for love to come and take her silent seat.
Patience holds the door for love. Love outsuffers any crime.
To purify oneself by love is the best use of time.

May 27

Fairy Tale

Let's relax for a minute, breathe in the belly, prevent
the lower self from setting his ambush. Body tension
accumulates and coils around the effort to be here,
wholly here, so we must be patient and intelligent.
It's a battle, yes, but more a contest of breath than blows.
Stretch out the crocodile, rub his underside; held in check
he'll be, and then we can dance and drink nectar and make love.

It's an odd life we have here – working like bees to prepare
for the sacrament of our own birth beside the great beast's
charmed slumber. It's a fairy tale, but one all too easy
to fall out of back into the human lie – the belief
that the next whatever will finally bring contentment,
and breath's just something occurring while thoughts
    secure the world.

May 28

Invitation

It takes terminal resolve to give one's thoughts no credence.
As what we know of life transpires in a thick cloud of thought,
we must be willing to die to leave it. Are you ready?

He wasn't sure why she was in the parade, but she smiled
as she passed and suddenly everything was different,
separate and clear. He walked the entire route beside her.

What's it worth to be what your life means? How long can you hold
the unnaming presence of this moment, not reclaiming
your place among the living dead who don't know that you're gone?

If you choose to drop all your baggage and ascend the air,
you will come to the end of names, where breath is pure rhythm
and the Angels apparent in their light will not shock you.

May 29

Get Up

It is the part of you that worships and pleads that must be
jettisoned. It's precisely what holds you down in the lie
of firm footing. Take off your shoes and let the sacred ground
drop away as you ascend to where height has no meaning.

A newborn babe will grip its father's finger confirming
its presence in a body. Now we seek the other way,
letting go of everything – fathers, ideas, senses –
confirming presence itself, unattached, even to us.

There is nothing else. Call it pure being, God, whatever,
then please stop talking. There is no other God before now.
You're on your knees because your lower self desires the dirt
and tricks your heart into believing you must beg God's love.

May 30

Passerby

The world agitates the heart; its abundant energy
surges and vibrates. For what will it be the fine fuel?
What will be strengthened, the soul's presence or the illusion
that one can change the world? Either choice is a submission.
Who is the master you would serve with your thundering heart?

Relieve suffering, but do not expect its extinction.
Challenge injustice, though you end up causing it elsewhere.
Demand your freedom, and your freedom will imprison you.
The lower self stands behind all attempts to change man's fate,
behind all belief in a lasting human victory.

Feed this hungry child because he is kneeling before you.
Free this battered slave because you cannot do otherwise.
Hold this oppressor's arm lest it strike that innocent one.
And through it all, let your heart feed the presence of your soul,
not the belief in your goodness. You are a passerby.

May 31

Ready

With enough time in the ring, one sees the punches coming.
Yes, believe it or not, one forgets where one is: fighting –
not desperately enough – for one's soul. And the punches
land, mostly on the body, and then one is retreating
and hurting and remembering to fight and retreating
and remembering and hurting. But sooner than before
one recovers and stands practicing the art one has learned
for just this situation, this moment. As the next punch
looms, I can see it, I see it, I'm here, hands up, ready.

§

June 1

Religion

If religion is the fossilized formula that Schools
decay into – revelation hardened into temples
swept with priestly garments – then not being present makes one
deeply religious and dead as the past. Forgetting prompts
beliefs, doctrines, pre-prayed sentiments, rules, and impatience
to get one's shoes back on. If you would abandon the mosque,
or leave the church, the best way is to remember yourself;
then you can converse with the Angels who only want you
here and present in the cathedral of the universe.

June 2

Coming In

Tired, worn perilously thin, ripped in spots too numerous
to mend: such is the sail, and the map shows no healing cove
to hide in. The watches are long, rest short, the provisions
strictly rationed. The flies and mosquitoes come from all sides
with their infected buzz. Each man's skin bears a colony
of ulcerations, and breathing – simple breathing – requires
the full mind. Such are the last weeks of this quest to be free,
to be no longer sailors of the world's uncertainty.

June 3

The Djed Pillar

That the djed pillar symbolizes stability makes
perfect sense to me now. It looks like the four vertebrae
low in the spine which keep a man upright and Heavenward
and prevent him from tottering when he walks. The serpent
in us seeks the ground, slithering beneath our awareness,
glad when we fall. But the simple djed provides firm support,
keeps the heart above the gut, and even allows a cross
to be carried over short distances. Angels want us
to transform their annihilating gaze, to look at them,
our backs unbent, our hearts engaged, our foreheads in the sky.

June 4

Crushed

The identity we form with our lives of flesh is wrong,
all wrong. It is dark and painful, full of obligation,
dependent on mirrors and imagined worth. To have it
shattered is a gift: it must not be permitted to stitch
and glue its image back together. It will lie its way
back to wholeness and dominion. God, crush it beyond thought.
Let rise in its place a loving transparent perceiver
moving over the world like a blessing no one can name.

June 5

This Realm

During long imprisonment, patience starts to grow in one,
and when its taproot has gone deep, and it breathes its own life,
one becomes less the imprisoned and more the dear witness.
These shifts of identity prepare one for true service –
to God, to mankind – and when the Angel comes through the door
and leads one out, the frightening price of going with him
is to sever one's attachment to the bars of free will.

June 6

Only in Time

Only in time do things matter; only in time must you
choose between good and evil, chocolate and vanilla,
Sally and Margaret. Only in time does the dog bite
become infected, and the food rot and the grass go brown.
Out of time, there is only love; love is all we can know
of eternity, whether we call it love or presence
or remembrance of God or awareness of attention.
It moves faster than light, and we stand in it transfigured,
while the much mattering world pounds its churn and death congeals.

June 7

Hugging the Night

A response that does not take a minute to formulate
is inadequately thought out, but the soul of a man
does not need that minute or any brain's instant of it.
It returns calls faster than a kicked doggy's shocked instinct
can bark the only bark it has. How do we confuse them,
the thinking machinery and the soul's lightspeed crystals?
Sometimes by thinking too much, sometimes by not listening...
Even when stars shoot through the sky, we doubt; we hug the night.
We really did see them, as the dog barked at the shadows.

June 8

Refugees

The old earthsuit is not restless or hungry or angry,
so it wants me to close my eyes to the sun and nod off.
Like puppies that will just be a nuisance, it is drowning
my thoughts and has turned to jelly all my best intentions.

What is will in this situation? To fight the creeping
torpor will only drain me further. Instead I'm writing
this poem, a few syllables, a few breaths at a time,
sneaking them onto the page, like scared refugees, alive
in a new land with nothing but their heartbeats to transform
their escaped self-awareness into the meaning of life.

June 9

Not Browsing

"Browsing in a field by night" – such are our best impulses
when left undirected and unsequenced, says Muhammad.
We must put them in close ranks for the solemn procession;
walk them step by breath up the nave, around the sacristy
until they attain the incandescence of withheld dance.

Thus Moses crossed the Red Sea, Christ traversed all Galilee,
cathedral craftsmen measured stone and light, and the small key
on the tail of Franklin's kite lit up all America.
Long has been our wait to walk in the gardens of this land.
Hands joined we move, purposeful not browsing, in steps of light.

June 10

G.T.O.

It's not self-deprecation to say I am a coward,
but neither is it always true; in some situations
I have the noblest courage and in others the wisest
indifference. What then am I? I will keep it simple.

See, I participate in the Great Twitching Organic,
the moving film of life that coats the planet and protects
its fragile function in the solar body. My species
is the mental element of that work and proud of it.
Thus is explained all my body does. The complexity
can fool you, but the big picture – the Great Twitching – is clear.

Yet something else I've come to be as well – no good to you
or man or the planet: an incognito spy, serving
Heaven, major domo at the mansion of no address,
the payer and the payment, purchasing myself for God.

June 11

Resting the Donkey

The body aches and ages, and being carried by it
is like riding an arthritic donkey over sharp rocks.
It's good sometimes to pause and have mercy on the poor beast:
Give it a rub and a brushing, but don't sit long and lax.
It will want to talk philosophy, give its reasoned thoughts
on the true location of Atlantis and tempt the mind
to places very uneconomical to travel.
Rest only briefly, mindful of the sun, and mount up soon.
Sing rhythmic songs that the creature can't resist joining in.

June 12

Knowing His Face

Driving before dawn this morning, I saw Death on the road
coming toward me but on the other side, the intention
on his face directed past me into the glazed distance.
I glanced and knew him but could not turn the full attention
of my being to him. There is my work, I thought, knowing
we would scuff shoulders once or twice before his gaze was fixed
upon me. I must know his face, his gait, his greeting kiss,
and ready a transforming hospitality to meet
the hollow knocking of his duty, so despised. Ah, yes! –
I forgot to tell you. He is young, not bent and toothless.
His hair is silky black, his posture aristocratic,
and the love of God informs his perfect unrelenting.

June 13

Quite a Trick

It's quite a trick not to be this aging, tired body.
One keeps it scrubbed, exercised, flushed with vitamins, doctored,
dressed in prescribed dignity, socially circulated,
insured, informed, housed comfortably among pretty things –
What will one not do for it? It's very easy to lose
oneself in all this providing, all this palace building,
and forget why one has the poor carcass in the first place:
to be transported by it, to be carried up the steps
in its obedient hands, past breath, to one's true being.

June 14

The Scale

Every moment is that weighing between heart and feather.
The heavy heart has no chance; down it sinks to the mud bank
to be swallowed whole by the river beast whose swollen belly
is its great delight. By renouncing, the heart can stay clean,
but the lift, the flight, it must get from its own surging, out
beyond earth's gravity to beauty known before bodies.
And of course the hand of God is always engaged, holding
the scale, the fulcrum a quarter inch in the heart's favor.
Why this grace? Why do you help your child who's trying his best?

June 15

Lemon Soap

When one is deeply present, one can feast on smells alone.
A rose is a banquet, a woman's perfume a session
of the most acute lovemaking. The bread in the oven
gives forth an ocean to sail on. But if one is enthralled,
it can take a torment of stinging to summon one back.
The skunked dog comes yelping toward home to be scrubbed, eyes too burne
to open. Get the lemon soap and bend to do your work.

June 16

How Sweet

What a luxury to have cool morning hours to oneself:
rising a little later – much less painful in the back;
extending one's walk with the dog that stops to sniff and play;
savoring the tea and reading carefully, gratefully
the sentences of well meaning men; then sitting with pen
and book in the poetry chair, writing this little verse
to you, reminding us both how sweet is simple being.

June 17

Till God is Ready

Shouldering the cross again, rising from the rocky ground –
the sweet, damning doze defeated – one stands to welcome death.
But death is coy. First a hundred splinters in the shoulders,
then a broken toe, an ankle sprained, the neck distended
and a weak hip wrenched from socket. "Believe, believe in me,"
cry out the nerves that quicken pain. "This agony is real!"
And so it is till God is ready for one's death and takes
the offering, leaving the wood, the nails, the flesh and blood.

June 18

In Your Constancy

It is not a good idea to overtax the heart's
enthusiasm. An overdressed eagerness to help
is just another vanity, the devil on the right,
hiding in goodness. Better for everyone if you stand
silently ready until you're asked to offer a word
of unassuming love, to raise a curtain six inches,
to move a water glass within easier reach. The soul's
striving can be subtle. In your constancy, your firm acts
of invisible love, do not fear insignificance.

June 19

No Doubt

Don't make it more than it is. The solemn and the sacred
hold society together, but for this single man
sitting in his chair, watching the window made of light
and breathing to the pulse of his attention, there is no need
for sacrament, no proof of holiness required, no doubt.

June 20

What's Left to Be?

Having found the Truth, having worn a reliable path
to its gate, you must with each trip back leave something mortal
in the woods until all that can die has been discarded.
The worthy steward is the last to go, as his mother's
compassionate tears are by then cried out. What's left to be
that the silence of Heaven has not eclipsed? God abides.

Summer

Summer --- God

> *It is by the grace of God that we recognize the grace of God.*
>
> *Petrarch*

> *Wherever you turn, there is God's face.*
>
> *The Koran*

June 21

Once One Knows Why

Once one knows why one is here in an earthsuit respiring;
once one has loosened the husk of identity and moves
around in it without fear of death or loss or failure;
once one has gotten out of one's own way, stopped impeding
all in one that desires nothing but to return to God;
then one's moments left on earth, whether one or many more,
are a sweet suffering, a stone's welcome to the bright stream
wearing it smooth, smoother, featureless, dissolved, gone to God.

June 22

Dancing

If you're thinking about your steps, you're no longer dancing.
Take your pick, dancing or thinking, being here or thinking,
making love to God or thinking. No thinker in right mind
would choose thought over God, so lock up that dangerous thing!

The thing I mean is a master of identity theft.
It calls itself you and is barricaded in your throat
where it talks to itself all day while holding the real you –
God's lover – hostage and forbidding all forms of dancing.

You must chase the thing out and down to its own snaky lair
and set a guard at the throat's gate, only allowing in
the high heart's best prayers. In no time, you'll be on the dance floor,
free of all false choices, twirling with God and no one else.

June 23

Smaller

Why does everyone want to be large, live in large houses,
make large fortunes and perform before large audiences?
Don't they get it? You only get larger rolling down hill.
Approaching the summit, you get smaller, just a bare speck
in the base camp's big binoculars. Becoming yourself
makes you smaller and smaller until it isn't yourself
you're becoming, until all that's down below can't reach you,
and you've disappeared, returned, into the silence of God.

June 24

Poetry

Invoking God, begging and thanking God, exalting God –
these can all be done in prayer and poetry like the Psalms;
but at some point, the poet must forsake his voice and leave
God to silence. For addressing God is not being God.

The poet's work consolidates the finest energy
of the best utterances formed in the best symmetries
in an invitation to be left leaning on God's door.
Having spoken, the poet must wait in air above words.

Like all the best human efforts, poetry navigates
restraints. Being God dissolves restraints, abandons limits,
vacates appearances and surrounds with endless silence
the poet's song. What means more to you, poetry or God?

If poetry, then quit writing and get out of God's way.
If God, leave your ongoing unsigned verses by the road.

June 25

History Now

The overlords of money are roiling the world again.
When all settles, we will be poorer, and more will agree
with what they've been told to think. The exhaustion that follows
fabricated crisis makes the herds more manageable.

Worrying about the latest apocalypse will prompt
your patient soul's hibernation. It can wait centuries.
History is not a bathtub whose depth and temperature
you control. It's an ocean. Leave it to the doomed captains.

Whether you survive or not is up to Higher Forces.
No plan of yours can guarantee it. Can you see the sky?
Can you and your loved ones share a small meal in fellowship?
Where's better to live, in your head or in God's deathlessness?

June 26

More of God

Thinking about being with God as a transport of light
and delight is, after all, still thought. With fine subtlety,
God is always here: the question is whether you are here.
If you are, then God is known, whatever poor thinking does.

The smallest taste is worth pursuing, worth dropping thought for,
and all your worry and vanity and expectation.
A single breath of remembering God – which is really
God's awareness of you – gives you life because it is life.

Sainthood and holiness are ideas. God is a state.
Do you desire more of God? Send your name home to supper.
Fan the desire to a flame with breath measured by the heart.
Hold attention with your love and love with your attention.
Now there's as much of God as loving emptiness can bear.
In truth, the borders have dissolved; in truth there's nothing else.

June 27

It's Your Attention

When the Eye of the soul is open, no matter what else
is going on, there is innocent delight abiding.
The problem is we get in the way of it, unaware
of anything else but the poor world's returning refuse.

Yes, your toe is infected and throbbing, your children sick,
your car held together by tape, your job in jeopardy,
your nation bankrupt, your air and water toxic. All true.
All life suffers. Earth is a prodigious pain factory.

That said, the delight of the open Eye is also true.
Your choice is not simply one or the other, but how much
each is attended. You may inhabit the pit of "I"
in which all the garbage ferments, or you may be elsewhere,
and rather than distort the soul's sight, become transparent.
Your toe is still going to smart, and the old tradition
of egotism will want to feed on the hurt. The flesh
is weak, but the love now here from God's open Eye is real.

June 28

Hospitality

It is a great paradox that God is here all the time
but so difficult to find. There is a reason for this.
God is not trying to be evasive or troublesome;
rather the problem is the conditions we insist on.

We want God to come to us, but the us we think we are
is imaginary. For example, look at the sky:
for half a brain's instant, there is God, but then thinking starts;
the mind gets going and the real vision evaporates.

The thing we call ourselves, the thing in imagination,
has turned away from God and demanded a miracle --
not hospitable terms for a meeting. We summon God
from our front porch, then run inside the house and lock the door.

Let's look at the sky again, and when imagination
begins its chatter, banish it. Let's not collude with it.
There's the real sky again, the inky mind clouds breaking up,
and God arrives, fully here, and there's nothing between us.

June 29

Welcome

Don't be insulted that I didn't seem glad to see you.
I was expecting God and thus forgetting the presence
that's always here. But now your arrival has brought me back,
and of course you too are a manifestation of God
as am I. The whole universe is God dispersed in time –
as us, as everything – reconnecting, remembering
the delight of being. So welcome here, friend, God now known.

June 30

Dance Partners

Wanting God is good; better to move intelligently
toward God step by step until surrender is possible.
The strength of surrender is key: God needs an empty space
to fill with being. Thus God created the universe
and each microcosmos too to complete with abundance.
We are already part of God, but until surrender
we don't participate. We stand along the wall waiting
to be asked to dance as if needing permission to be.

§

July 1

Unexpectation

Sometimes in a rush of pure attention, the mind empties
for an instant and one is sucked out through the little cleft
in time that has been inadvertently made. Come to prize
these moments. Learning to create them is worth your whole life.
When one happens, let go of everything. Hold the nothing,
and see the now unveiled truth before you with certainty.
If you have sufficient presence, God will kiss your forehead,
a charming affirmation for even the dearest friend.

July 2

Spent History

History cannot continue at this speed. It will lose
all discrimination and disintegrate into shards
no one knows how to value. Everyone will be urgent
to survive, but few will face the truth of how to do it.
There will follow a long dying, a general decrease
while the new dispensation gestates in its blue cocoon.

Where are you in this picture? Your closet is full of clothes.
Do you have a garden plot, a well, seeds, the love of friends?
Do you know how to transform time to eternal presence?
Do you know how to make a soul from events large and small?
Civilizations rise and fall: they have their own clear scope
which men in self-righteous vanity think they influence.

Let the body work as it was made to do; let the mind
return to simplicity. Where is your attention now?
The one aware of the answer to that question is God.
Be with God as much as you can, as deeply as you can.
Make the rest of you a true shrine with your heart as its priest.
Spent history must rest; the only rest for man is God.

July 3

This Looks Like A Poem

This looks like a poem, but it's not, and neither is it
just a collection of ink strokes on a page. It's a drop
of God, just as we are. If we must get more specific,
this small verse is God's reminder given to me for you
that we are all one in God and eventually all
our remembering of ourselves leaves nothing left for time.
Till then, may the illusion of being other than God
not be too unpleasant. If your mind must have a poem,
here are ten fourteen syllable lines by, for, from, to God.

July 4

The Fence

God lives just beyond that fence, the one we built in the dreams
we call our lives. Every thought believed, everything we take
credit for, every fear that keeps us standing here hoping
adds more wire to the fence. And our nerves electrify it.

Whether yours, mine or anyone's, it's called the fence of "I,"
and one has to get over or through it to get to God.
True, God could visit this side and occasionally does,
but God figures you built the fence and so waits patiently.

So how does one get past the fence that one's own mind has made?
You must see that thinking about it is not the best way;
in fact, just the opposite: one has to let go of thought –
all its posts and nails. Then what happens to identity?

The "I" becomes less real, more a social convenience.
At some point an opening appears (it was always there).
One walks right through, and the whole division of I and God
vanishes, and all that's left is the great feast of return.

July 5

You

You've probably been in a spot where what you think you are
had lost all control and something other worldly kicked in:
The car careening, the brakes unresponsive, the collision
a relentless vision speeding into being despite you;
or the handle of the saw slipping by its own will out
of a hand unavailable to your brain's screaming commands;
and then silent, timeless watching by a state unafraid,
a deathless peace overruling all your mortal panic.

But because you still want to be you, the thing that survived,
you attribute that bizarre experience to something
outside yourself – God, or an Angel overwatching you,
but you don't dare press the thought to sacrilegious space:
that the God who appeared was you, the real you, not the you
you wear everyday, but the eternal you that is God.
No, you'd rather think some great spirit loves the you you know.
Sorry, that you returns to the dirt, not ready for God.

July 6

I Must Be Patient

I must be patient and remember how slow the work is.
When I offer it to someone who has delighted me
with his sincerity and honest questions, I want him
instantly in Heaven, blossomed past the threshold of time.

I forget that he must accumulate many millions
of tiny recognitions, molecules of new vision,
before he knows himself steadfastly, before he becomes
the one true God rejoining all of us welcoming him.

July 7

Poor Shackled Thought

No thought reaches high enough, and when it reaches as high
as it can, thought hurts itself and whines. Better not to think,
but to be aware of attending the forehead of God
at which poor shackled thought lunges and snarls,
    fawns and whimpers.

July 8

Beauty

Beauty is in the Eye of God; when you, O beholder,
and God are one, then beauty can be in your eye as well.

The lower self dominates by closing everything down.
Imagination constricts the breathing and the senses –
sticks the tongue to the palate, locks the jaws, glazes the eyes –
and pretty soon the heart and mind have become exclusive,
and the person prejudiced, possessive, paranoid, proud.

But higher emotions begin by opening, stretching,
letting the heart expand in full flower, disburdening
the mind of all it thinks it knows, unblocking the breathing,
allowing the unrestricted being of everything
and seeing everything as it is in tender focus.

So if you want beauty, be God, openly loving all
the senses offer, softly with your Eye praising their praise.

July 9

Flexed

The thickened tongue can hold one stuck in imagination;
the eyes glaze and seal one in the bleak bubble of belief.
There's a physical component, a complex posturing
to our sleep. The denial of reality requires
a flexed effort, a closing down to God's ongoing gift.

July 10

Bird Without A Call

There is a bird without a call whose colorless feathers
and nestless travelings leave it unknown to all but those
who have learned that its gaze is the only way to find it.
You must gaze as it gazes – unexpectant watchfulness
wanting nothing but to witness the manifestations
of God. Gaze this way, train the Eye, and the bird will be here.

July 11

Ears

Prayer works by preventing imagination. One cannot
imagine oneself if prayer occupies the narrow gate;
the lying words and pictures can't get through, and God's mercy
provides for sincere prayer to always have the right of way.
So why does praying stop? The steward gets tired and becomes
subject to error and distraction, disoriented
into thinking he's someone else with something else to do.
God has nothing else to do but be God, but what are we?
Highjackers storming the gate? Heroes with their upraised swords?
Lovers putting prayers in God's ears? Or just the ears themselves?

July 12

Ah!

Humid, tranquil and warm is this day, like inside a womb,
and all I want to do is rest. How ignoble it is
to withdraw and leave the suffering to the idiots –
or is it? Who can it be in this hammock next to mine?
Ah! It's God! Whoever would guess I'd discover you here!

July 13

The Mail

Writing a poem's like sitting down to open the mail.
There are a few bills to pay (one can't have mail without bills),
announcements of new ventures and partnerships, temptations
offered at a discount to test one's good sense and resolve,
and frequently a surprise love note from God to enjoy:
"Where have you been? All is forgiven. Waiting here for you."

July 14

Born

Please don't make God hurt you any more than necessary.
The amniotic bubble you won't leave must be broken
and you dragged from the darkness of thought,
   your clutched throat opened
to the current of love longing to navigate from your heart
to your forehead and up through the crown to waiting Heaven.

These things must occur. The illusion that you are not God
can be tolerated only so long before it kills
all your sacred memories. Don't prolong the suffering.
Don't cling to the things you've gathered down here. Leave everything
you've acquired to the dirt scavengers who know no better.

Your reluctant thoughts alone will feed them quite long enough
for you to be forgotten and born to eternty.

July 15

Walking the Path

Just walking the path regularly with sincerity
will compact the earth, make it too firm for the weeds to grip.
If you're weak, the devil makes you wonder why. If you're strong,
he beseeches you to demonstrate how. If you've beyond
weak or strong, you just walk, not listening to his questions.
And one day the light from the sky meets the light reflected
from below right at the balcony of the soul, and earth
holds you up as you emerge from all the fake inquiries
and vain answers to get your great assignment face to face.

July 16

Ring The Bells

Angels ring their bells in my ears. God is here, they proclaim.
Release the words from your throat, the furrows from your brow.
Empty the chalice of your heart to fill it up with God.
The prayer of the Eye's awareness is answered: God is here.
Levitating above the crown of the head, God is here.

July 17

Always and Everywhere

Whatever you're doing right now, whatever you're doing
anytime at all, God's cameras are rolling, getting
it all for the record. It isn't like God wants to build
a vast library of human business. Not at all.
It's just part of the price God has to pay to create us.
As God is eternally conscious, God can't forget us,
even for a moment. The cameras, the library –
all metaphors. The real truth: God, always and everywhere.

July 18

Just As Now

You're breathing to it. It's where you're sitting, what you're seeing.
It's the view of your thoughts in procession across your mind.
It's the first ever, the only. There's no future in it.
If you could just be, you'd be it. It's so easy to lose,
and life depends on finding it: that is, finding ourselves
and disappearing into it. All for you, here it is.
Wherever you go, tie memory to it, just as now.

July 19

Even It

You can mate in an earthsuit, but the soul remains locked in,
unable to merge through the filters of flesh and psyche.
It's the suit's coupling, not the soul's. Imagine having sex,
each wrapped in heavy blankets with hoods, goggles and earplugs.
Souls mate in the ether, which for us is a state – presence,
and that kind of mating occurs across time and distance.

There's another kind of merging – when the soul discovers
that even it is a veil and surrenders to being
beyond the earthsuit's instruments, complete in God's nothing.

July 20

Higher

So subtle the immortal part that does not need to speak.
I mean not the Eye and its blisses, but the Crown, barely
kissing the skull – at all things unperturbed, weightlessly perched.
In air too fine for breathing, it is too aware for earth
to stain, and everything that it observes is clarified.

What is its secret of being? It knows itself deathless
and wisely yields all mortal things their troubled passages.
It does not need or want and has nothing to show, no thoughts,
no hope, its transparent love refined to pure allowing.

It is an invisible bird, alert without tension,
levitating above the mind's metaphors and its prayers.

July 21

Being Human

If you were waiting, now might be the time to claim your bright
birthright – that is, the precious reward of being human.
Don't be fooled by the willingly blind: humans are special,
and great it is to be born one. Even a short, crippled,
coughing, homely and irritable human life has gold
in its Eye and its fitted Crown. So claim it. Lift it up
from the shoetop shelf of tired things to the knees of belief,
past the snaky swamp and the waste of waist, to feed the heart.
Then let the nourished heart report, but keep it a secret
and whisper it in the cupped ear of God, who never tires
of hearing from the beloved human experiment.

July 22

Bold Action

Take bold action and don't look back; don't look forward either.
The past and the future are illusory; we use them
to schedule appointments, to grow crops, to conquer the earth,
but we cannot base identity on them: time bodies
are not souls. What we truly are remains untouched by time,
so the action you must boldly take is to be. Look up!

Hoist yourself out of the current of time, get a footing
on the bank of the present, stand, grip mindfulness, let go
of everything that beats itself in panic or resents
being taken from some imagined tournament. The rest
is what you are, a divine offering returned to God.

July 23

The Song in Your Ears

Here's what to do when you have no chance of sex or money
or food or applause: you listen to the poem Heaven
has put here in front of you to utter. Come inside out
with me! Break your head open! Let your thoughts disintegrate!

Die to your fat life of pleasures repeated unto death.
Burst into the blossom God longs for you to be. No one's
looking, and the song in your ears right now is immortal.

July 24

We Die And Die

What is death? The earthsuit damaged past use or just worn out.
Luckily, it's biodegradable. The soul is freed,
and depending on the illusions it has taken on,
goes here or there for purification – sometimes ages –
until it no longer takes life personally. Praise God.

Death is the end of an opportunity for the soul
to strengthen against the weighty resistance of the flesh
with the aim being to become clearly, permanently
itself, a principle in the mind of God, witnessing
everything's return. So we die and die until bodies
aren't necessary anymore and welcomed is what is.

July 25

Bad Deal

Bad deal! Here's Heaven all around and you settle for thoughts.
Pull your tongue off the roof of your mouth and let the honey
your heart has made ascend to the balcony on your brow!
You are not mankind. You have no duty to the species.
You are not Atlas letting the rude planet crush your neck.
You owe nothing, and if there isn't another earthsuit
in a thousand miles, those that truly love you are with you
in eternity. Enjoy your awareness. Take delight
in being. Take it! As you become love, you'll want to share
yourself with other prisoners, and thus you will extend
the cord of God. It's not an idea, not a duty.
Your jealous, guilty groping can't grasp what you truly are.
Be silent! Right here in front of you is God's attention.

July 26

Wake Up

What ripe poem will God commit to us today, dear hearts?
The singing words provoke the dance of conscious sentiency,
and we turn inside out with love and shock to suddenness
the drooping ears of the napping world. We wake and listen!

July 27

The Ringing

The ringing in my ears used to be sporadic, but now
it is constant. It can be drowned out by louder noises
but it is still here, a current driving my awareness.
I am grateful for it. It distracts me from distraction,
and it's better than pain. Like everything the last few months,
it reminds me of God, who is also now always here.
Consciousness emerges and rises above the ringing,
the ringing, the ringing; it gathers to smooth attention,
then shakes hands with God and steps back into silent service,
unresisting the ringing. No need to change anything.

July 28

Accidents

Accidents change things, but only for the mind, not for God.
The content of the next moment is just a likelihood
for us, but for God whatever can happen is not change.
So if you want to be like God, you must become past all
becoming, speak unto silence, let the last wave of breath
wash you up on nowhere, your heart full of divine nothing.

Here's a change – a new line of verse. Is God different now?
Your next thought arcs across your mind. Is God different now?
The world ends again and again. Is God different now?
As you retreat, God fills the space of always everywhere.

July 29

The Proof

Can I will the state that writes this poem? No, I cannot,
but I can invite it with my surrender, offering
up everything I want from this experience, all that,
in order to have the experience itself, all this.
What can I offer God after all but my departure?
I vacate the space to be visited, and God arrives
with miraculous regularity, bringing poems.
By tempering amazement at God's will, my own will grows.
This is the proof, brought and left here for me to give to you.

July 30

Out And Back

A dozen vultures high in a digger pine attending,
and one higher still. Out and back they glide in two's and three's,
checking, checking again: a feast prepares itself for them.
In the long gulley below my house, something is dying.

Who has made this gathering? Is it Heaven's instruction,
or an allegory that my state projects on the screen
of the world? Why does the perfect order so confound me?
I am all of this, and the illusion of its meaning,
and the God playing with the mind trying to contain it.
Be, observe, observe, be. What we are here strains to nothing.

July 31

This

Make a great pile: your money, your clothes, your knowledge, your thoughts.
Leave everything you have on the floor in front of her gaze.
The charmed woman weaving sound and silence into music
is not the soul, but with her barely upturned lips she'll give
the cherished signal that you're free to climb the final stair
to this roofless room of presence to meet the soul you are.
Of course God's here. What else is the soul but this awareness?

§

August 1

Desireless

The soul can only desire one thing: submission to God.
All other wants are from the body. Cleverly disguised
or nakedly demanding, the desires of the body
come down to the trinity of pleasure, status and stuff.
God also appears as a trinity, but the desire
to submit understands in its mindfulness beyond mind
that God is one, nothing you can think of and all there is.

August 2

Devoured

Taking delight in the mind is risky: the irony
of our condition can be distilled into a proud drug,
a nepenthe so powerful that whole philosophies
can be derived from it. In the end, death devours the mind,
but its clever, ironic waste can stink for centuries.

So what's the antidote? God's love. (Feel the proud intellect
recoil at the mere phrase.) The truth also works – the real truth,
not the ironic truth: the truth of the present moment.
It's always best to begin with presence, the state beyond
words, thoughts – all mind things. As surrendering to the present
completely, unconditionally, will invite God's love,
you (now gone to God) won't mind feeling your proud mind devoured.

August 3

The Conditions

When the serpent constricts the breath, closing the gate to God,
imagination begins. Inner talk and picturing
capture us, and the sealed-off world becomes the darkened realm
of the lower self. Most human beings live and die there.

The steward is aware of breath, holding open to God,
patiently refining readiness, devoting himself.
Will God come? Will the blessing of clarity arrive now,
revealing what has always been, is and will always be?

When God presides, the body is a pedestal for the Eye,
blessing the earth with its gaze; the Crown a lens to observe
and temper the abundant love lest the swelling heart burst.
All is God, that which breathes in time and that which breath exalts.

August 4

Balancing Loves

Earthsuits age, droop and shrivel; they become unattractive,
revolting to touch or imagine touching, death to kiss.
But what of the soul using the suit or the child within?
How do these untouchables give and receive affection?

The separate soul keeps its earthsuit cleaner than in youth.
Intimate with God, it can endure the body's longings.
But the child does not understand either age or the soul.
The child reaches to embrace and kiss freely from the heart.
And even a wrinkly earthsuit will vibrate and straighten
in passionate delight sometimes, forgetting how it looks.

It's a problem keeping these skills and limitations clear:
being the soul remembering God, letting the child breathe,
keeping the suit's cravings from poaching on eternity.
Balancing all this love opens the door of our escape.
The Angels have sympathy for this plight and will visit;
you'll get support; and as you're discrete, God keeps your secrets.

August 5

If You Can

Tension and release – such is the rhythm and pulse of life.
Are you mounting to a peak or descending to a trough,
ascending to sky or falling back to earth? Up and down
we go; identification – the lower spine gripping
the heart which obeys by believing and losing all scale –
is inversely proportional to the presence of God.
Individual organisms grow, mature and die;
species come and go; organic life waxes and wipes out.

Let it all go, even, if you can, the lower spine's hold
which only love and terror can command; let it all die;
let whatever you think you are disperse. The breathing thing
isn't you. Witness and wait till waiting isn't waiting.
Be mindful, no longer mind. Nameless. Pure awareness. Now.

August 6

Certainty

Certainty is not a condition of logical mind.
Certainty is the elevation that presence provides
to the soul. At its firmest, it's an indestructible
rock of self-awareness that no crashing wave of the sea
of illusion can move. It dresses real identity
when one withdraws from the blending data of the senses.
Certainty watches over the whole humming hologram
of world and self, a vantage above, a lens for the last
witnessing of creation before God's dissolving gleam.

August 7

All God Wants

Having arrived, all God wants is you standing in witness,
holding attention as the presence suffuses the air
you're breathing, your braincase empties its chattering concerns
and your heart opens and spills, drowning all your own desires.
Into the pure vacancies of your being God will pour
presence, and the membrane of identity will weaken
and finally give way into the all and everything.

August 8

When You Are God

When you pray, does it strike you that you're talking to yourself?
Why not be God, whose being is the answer to all prayer?

Remember, God is not "out there." Nirvana, Paradise,
the Kingdom of Heaven, Samadhi, God – they're all within.
You already participate in God, and the more so
the greater the self-awareness you kindle and sustain.
So instead of your prayers being petitions supporting
your little self's view of how it prefers the world to be
("Please, God, don't let Mama die, and let there be no more wars."),
better be God: let the spark of God within fully flame,
take you over, consume your eyes and your heart and your name.

When you are God, you won't need to ask for things. Your being
will enfold the world in the deathless love beyond desire.

August 9

Be Next To Me

Be next to me, God, and let me slowly melt into you;
let the mindstuff that I'm made of unravel and disperse.
You are the awareness that remains, unbounded being.

The struggle of a living thing to live serves your purpose,
as does the submission unto death, the end of struggle.
I will labor in time to return out of time to you.

At last I am the only thing obstructing perfect love;
I have let go every property, every right and claim.
Now to surrender to the light, unweighted wonder be.

August 10

Drop

Drop the whole brain barrow of hot concerns over the cliff,
and it's as if the earthsuit's every cell screams and scrambles
for a new magnet of identity, a nucleus
warm to swarm around. The flesh cannot bear being nothing.

But nothing is precisely the way through, the chance to leave
the dense ganglia of false alarm wired around our names.
Drop it all. Be nothing now, and in that bare brain's instant
of silence before panic recovers, escape to God.

August 11

Becoming God – I.

Blake called God, the bearded power figure, "Nobodaddy,"
and some today, including the atheists, reference
the idea of an external God controlling things
as a "sky-daddy," a metaphor mocking the poor minds
that need an authority to petition and obey.

But as you know by now, God is not outside but inside;
that is, you are inside of God yet find God by looking
within you, and if you look bravely, all the divisions
between you and God and between God and everything else
will dissolve and render you, God and everything all one.

August 12

Becoming God – II.

How does one begin to experience and become God?
First clean the room. Sweep out all the heart's old prejudices,
the fixed ideas, the stiff-necked opinions, the grudges,
the sentimentalities, the culture of right and wrong,
all doubts, collusions, secret fancies. This may take a while.

While doing this, begin another front: become aware
of your attention – what your eyes see right here before you,
what your ears hear, what thoughts are arising and parading
across your mind, what movements and emotions are quickened
by those thoughts. Let these things exist as if apart from you.

Once you isolate yourself as the thing aware of all
the contents of your mind and senses, you can be truly
said to know yourself. You are not the swift flood surging there:
you are the awareness of that river of impressions,
rising to walk across to the other shore's purer air.

August 13

Becoming God – III.

Moments in that purer air consolidate, and slowly
we realize a new identity is being made
in a new dimension. We go and come back, elevate
then descend back to time and space, till the awakening
progressively occurs: we are souls in eternity.

Not a hope or a belief, this is an understanding
distilled from repeated experience, and our earth life
finds new purpose in supporting this great transformation.
On the globe of earth is built a square aligned to the stars
with sides ascending to a single point then vanishing.

And what was "I" becomes infinite, absorbed in conscious
totality. What can this be but God, the mind of God?
And the earth has its part; the availing bodies, their thoughts
and cravings, have theirs; and everything perfectly belongs
transformed in love proportionate to conscious letting be.

August 14

August

The heat of August takes all tension from the joints, leaves one
limp and listless, the fork unliftable, mail unopened,
buttons too complex. Night croakers don't bother anymore.
From Heaven rain down the meteors, merciless shrapnel
from blasts before mankind, leaving scratches on the lovers
in the dark where they've gone to be alone only to find
everyone else hiding, measuring their own endurance.

All our hiding from the frenzied sky of August can be
our unity, but such is a beggar's consolation.
Far better to understand that the Angels will not trust
us with any suffering we cannot transform. Our hearts
can make defiant, comforting love from each breath stolen
from the paralyzed air; our souls can quicken to beauty
in the needling night skies. We are not helpless to find God
undisturbed, welcoming us to join the eternal watch.

August 15

Relentless Mercy

Observing with the Eye of God, one sees the character
one's enacting in the great play, one sees the lower self
struggling for worldly advantage, one sees the illusion
of mortality and the torment of identity.

Only this vision allows true understanding of life.
Without it, reason is left to scavenge sporadic scraps
of truth, unconnected puzzle pieces which don't explain
the loss, the futile heartsongs, the abandonment in time.

Seeing as God sees, one must love poor longing humankind
and know that only by returning to eternity
can one help the Angels in their dire, relentless mercy
on our kindred, vessels of souls that do not know themselves.

August 16

Here All Along

Don't wait. God will catch up. It's better to get the cleaning
and quickening done. You don't need God to light the candles,
sweep the aisles, get the choir breathing right or start the prayers.

And you don't need God to open your heart. Your piety
and gratitude are yours. God doesn't need them, but you do.
An energized humility is also yours to bring.

When the choir's pure harmonies warm every inch of the walls
and ceiling, and the whole space is one incandescent mind,
God will visit, and the glory of presence will be known
and bring the understanding that God's been here all along.

August 17

Training The Puppy

The mind is the earthsuit's puppy, restless, moving, always
falling in something and forgetting all and everything.
Luckily it can be trained, but only God can do it.
The amazing thing is, God will. Yes, God will train your mind.

Heel your mind to heed God; drag it back each time it wanders
off to talk to itself in private or sniff up the skirt
of some fantasy. Make it sit here attentive to God,
right here, looking up with God's face directly before it.

It will take time. Of course, God could do it in an instant,
but it's dangerous and the results less reliable.
Again luckily, God is patient; every time you bring
the mind to God, a little trace of consciousness remains.

Thus is the mind trained, that is, brought to its utmost working:
the constant remembrance of God and the will to stay home.
Then it will be a good servant, protecting you from thieves
and mendacious vagrants who crave your precious attention.

August 18

Blessed

The current of nervous energy from the sacral spine
to the Eye and Crown is flowing uninterruptedly
this morning. I am alive and content. The faculties
which transcend a human scale and will make one an Angel
are operating perfectly through no effort of mine.

Such are the blessings of Angels: they reveal higher worlds
but keep our access in their hands. I breathe in certainty
of things over which more saintly men dissolve into doubt,
though my own will stumbles along in weak unworthiness.
Standing in Heaven, my knees bend in compassion for man.

August 19

Yes, Here Too

Let me remind you, God is here. Don't be superstitious.
If you don't feel the presence, make the needed adjustments
in your heart's attention. Drop the loud, interrupting thoughts.
Leave all the things that start with "I" stacked beside the fireplace.
Climb the vines to the balcony. (Or just use the ladder.
It's exactly where you left it.) Ease over the railing.
Step into the scented bedchamber and turn on the light.
Do you see now? Here's God. Yes, here too, everywhere you turn,
and you in your astonishment and me in mine, all God.
Breathe God gently in, and out, though God never really leaves.

August 20

Between The Worlds

As Rumi noted, the heart translates the miraculous
into the cruder fiber the mind can file. The heart moves
between the worlds, speaking compassion to the bewildered
and finding entrance to the court of God without the noise
of knocking. It's a trusted messenger whom God welcomes
as a man welcomes a quietly delighted lover.

August 21

A Lock On The Heart

There's an old lock on the heart that only God can open.
If you think there's no God, you're dying of thought, breathing blocked.
See, the lock restricts you to your head, keeps your sense of "I,"
and thus the whole universe, a thought thing. And what is thought?
It's the ever recycled past: wherever you move it,
however you refine it – down to pure math – it's not now.

It's a tragic loss for the soul that you're stuck in your head
with an idea of God you've made from your own poor past.
God is not an idea: not a stern, bearded daddy,
or a clockmaker, or a monkey at a typewriter.
All you can know of God is beyond thought. At that threshold,
the heart unlocks: the "I" of thought dies in the Eye of God.

August 22

Tea Garden

Marvelous as a tea garden in the midst of a slum
is a mind rightly serving the soul. The fountain issues
constant prayers, and all greetings, looks, smiles and meditations
ride gently on the bubbles, the syllables arising
to enrich attention. Carefully brewed and strained, the tea
is taken in sips, savored on the tongue. The eyes brighten,
and what is seen rests in light visiting on its journey
back to God. A crystal of being will grow and connect,
a portal out of time's abrasive rush. Keeping all thoughts
at bay, the mind in homing silence trusts a higher sky.

August 23

High Noon

As I come out from under the eve, the brighter than bright
morning sun shocks my eyes and brain, producing a terror
I must not shrink from but find nourishing, a source of love
I must bear and become worthy of. There is no more time
to shadow-play a life. The ecstasy of destruction
comes at high noon: God undisguised, boundaries vaporized,
all sleep annihilated, nothing left that is not God.
This cup must not pass away. No other road. No more words.

August 24

Mall Walking

Mall walking with the seniors. How ridiculous I look
to any eyes from any angle. How happy I am!

I stop for a moment to admire shoes in a display.
From behind and above the presence of God can be felt.
A message descends and collects language: "Yes, even this."

I walk again. Soon another grain of God's attention
crosses the border of time and mind and falls into words.
"Perfection waits on you. It is always present." Yes, this.

This earthsuit among the others continues its circuits,
content to be moving and breathing. Yes, even this. Yes.

August 25

Encounter

How do we know God? Follow this thought a ways. When you try
to remember yourself, the earthsuit's every stitch contracts
and resists your great step back. What dissolves that resistance
and lets you out to breathe and bathe in real air for a while?
It may be prayer or the Teacher's reminder or beauty
finding its way through your eyes to offer help to your heart.
When that neutralizing force is purely nothing, no thing,
you have encountered God in the perfect present. Hush now.

August 26

Home

Finally home, clenched and rigid from the day, I commit
to nothing, sweet nothing, to nobody and namelessness
and minutes unmeasured in their melting. "Do you love me?"
asks my puddle-eyed dog from her sofa. "Only so long
as you remain a dog," I reply with a master's glance,
my last artificial act of the day. God is coming.
Aware of what the Eye is seeing, I patiently wait
on the arrival – a few breaths, a year, a century,
however long God takes to reclaim all and everything.

August 27

Language

The problem with writing about God is that God's presence
so overwhelms the mind and heart that poems just intrude.
One hazards losing God in reporting the miracle.
Poetry works ably to render the ascent to God
and the descent to earth, but the peak is shrouded in clouds.

But what would happen were I face to face with God, trembling
in the present wonder, and God ordered me to compose
a verse for you? I doubt I could squeeze one idiotic
syllable out, much less a line of beautiful language.
And sure, God has now arrived to make me call my own bluff.

My brain is flooding with light, my heart with love for you all.
These are words, words. Use them as food if you can get them down.

August 28

Find The Point

It takes an Angel's help to hold attention on the thing
right in front of you; you resist and want to move your eyes
to the clouds, your hand to the phone, or your knees to the dirt.
But if you hold on as Menelaus held Proteus,
you'll be amazed at what will be revealed at nose's end.

All the Angel wants is for you not to miss God's presence,
and as it is right here where your slightly crossed eyes converge,
there's no reason not to partake in its joy. Clouds, phones, dirt,
dogs, churches, children, sex, money and all else the earthsuit
sustains in illusory orbit of itself can wait.

Find the point right before you, the still point. Relax your neck.
Surrender your attention to the Angel's direction.
Don't worry how you look with your eyes crossed. Between the brows
will come the softest tremor, and you will feel a transport
into God's vestibule. Whereto from here is up to God.

August 29

Goodness

Goodness is the desire to know God. Whenever you try
to figure out and then do the good thing, you really want
to return to the presence of God, which something in you
knows to be complete being – content, fulfilled, desireless.

Now doesn't it make sense that from the state of knowing God
you'll do what is good? So how do you arrive at that state?
All you have to do is remember God's presence. That's all.
Goodness, consciousness. Always, everywhere. Remember, God.

August 30

Only One

The body, which includes the mind, determines how the world
will appear to us and what we're worth in it. When joints ache,
we devalue dancing. Contrasting your body to mine
keeps us thinking in the illusion there are two of us.

Knowing the body – its lapses, pleasures and proportions –
we can subtract ourselves from it – let it be over there.
Self-awareness is a distillate, the presence still here
after all the fleshy forms and fumes have been flamed away.

Our confinement in mind confined in flesh bores God. Don't think
we can rely on God's mercy visits or bail money.
The body deteriorates: it must be forgiven.
There will be other bodies, but there is only one God.

August 31

Out Of The Way

If you would be with God, try being God being with you.
You'll see that being God is the easy part. All it takes
is complete surrender to what is. On the other hand,
you're heavy and make a big shadow, and being with you
may be simply too much to ask. Settle for just being.
Once you're out of the way, the whole universe opens up.

§

September 1

Knowing and Being

What we don't know is nearly everything. Perhaps that's why
knowledge is so seductive to humans: we'll kill for it.
But in our age, knowledge has been cheapened and diluted
to mere information and commoditized as content
for the global hypnosis – just something to think about.

If we knew ourselves, we'd see that we too are virtual.
That in us that is real is not us; identifying
with the organism, we forget about seeing God
face to face and settle for lives nose to screen. Are you there?
Can you read this line of type aware that you're reading it?

A great exercise is removing all the things not you --
the roles you play – to see what's left: professional, parent,
spouse, gendered thing, body.....Don't stop till you get to "being."
What do you know? You're a being. You are. An awareness.
The rest drops away, and here you are face to face with God.

September 2

The Better Best

In every moment, people are doing the best they can.
For us to do better in the next moment, becoming
more conscious is required. How do we become more conscious?

How does the screaming parent feel the damage to the child?
How does the deadly soldier quit being an enemy?
How does a human sense the poison of hidden hatred?

Action proceeds from states, better action from higher states.
On our small scale, the meaning of "the Lord our God is one"
is that only one state guarantees a loving action.

Love proceeds from the awareness of God; that awareness
arises in each moment we remember God's presence.
The best we can: this moment, the next, remembering God.

September 3

Not Believing

Trying not to believe your own thoughts is like expecting
to keep your feet dry as you stand on the beach with a wave
rushing in. You are quickly overwhelmed in soggy shoes.

Better to start with a small experimental planting
of not knowing. If you can bring this tiny crop to harvest,
you can slowly expand till not knowing dominates
your holdings and covers everything to the horizon.

Once a whole plantation of not knowing is established,
it's easier to not believe each day's variations
in the weather, the events in your household, or the thoughts
in your head. The lower self's alarms become much less shrill.

Through all this, it's crucial to recall that not believing
isn't disbelieving. Disbelieving and believing
are really the same false certainty, fueled by desire –
the lower self burning emotion to defend its turf.

Oddly, only not knowing and not believing can make
the earth firm enough to support true certainty, which comes
with the presence of God. Take off your shoes and know this state.

September 4

Being and Thought

If the first step is surrender, to what does one submit?
If one does not know God, how can one make a proper bow?

Honest questions of a mind trapped in thought.
    Thought seen as thought,
not as an identifying power, can simply be
steered off to the roadside, unblocking the way for being.

But one thought believed quickly gathers a loud entourage,
a mob whose noise drowns out simple being. Simple being
doesn't satisfy thought, but it's just to simple being
we must bow. When we do, God is here, ready to be known.

September 5

The Triangle

The dog is asleep on the sofa, the upholstery
protected by an old bedsheet. She makes no demands, breathes
languidly, doesn't care about the poem I'm writing
to you. It's very satisfying to reach out for you
without the world's interfering, without the world's urgent
noise and its lies. And if you respond by remembering
God, and remembering God again, then the triangle
from me to you to God to me to God to you to me
will be completed above time and space, and sleeping dogs
in your world and mine will remain undisturbed and docile,
floating down the great current of breath that we row upward
in our newly launched boat of forever: the Triangle.

September 6

The Wound

I am speaking to you and you know it. Don't make these lines
a conceit, a rhetorical device you can study
from a safe distance and be amused at its rich effects.

No, this poet is a sniper with your soul in his sights,
and the bullet's already been fired and is entering
your shocked self-awareness and assassinating your sleep.

You can try to backtrack into what you were, but the wound
of consciousness is open now, and there's nothing for you
but to collapse into God and surrender all your names.

September 7

Sacred Texts

Why do I study sacred texts? To learn the poetry
of submission. The soft prompting to prayer too often met
a stiff neck refusing to bow to God's clear beckoning.
I was so proud of learning remembering that I failed
the test of the present; only now can I surrender
to the breath of being, bending my forehead to God's breast.

September 8

Little Girl

What made her joy so great that her thoughts flooded out and quit
firing altogether, that her mouth burst like too ripe fruit
into a dripping smile, and without needing to do it,
her whole body understood the energy of dancing?

What caused this miracle? In an instant eternally
recorded, she caught high in the bright sky the Eye of God
monitoring the universe, and she saw herself there
in God's Eye, and knew at light speed that she was part of it
and it of her, and all the fragments were one shining thing.

And knowing this, she opened and let her tidy, puzzled
mother wipe with quick hands the juices dribbling down her chin.

September 9

What Do We Mean?

What do we mean when we say 'God'? I think we mean three things.
First we use the word to indicate the ineffable –
that which can't be named or thought though the word 'God'
   points to it.

Or we mean the 'God-man': a Krishna, a Moses, Buddha,
Jesus or Muhammad, who, depending on the culture,
is God's human form or son or friend or chief messenger.
This figure one models to rule one's internal cosmos.

But as we're reminded, both of these Gods are cursable:
We can deny them, stone them, stab them, chase them out of town,
and gaping hell still might not swallow us. We only fry
if we curse the Holy Spirit – the third meaning – the state
of being God, the wordless state for which the God-man gives
his life in sacrifice and which alone is perfect proof.

September 10

The Name of the State

You don't have to call God, "God." "God" is a word referring
to the phenomenon of presence, the self-aware state
in human experience. Nothing here to be believed
or worshipped. Drop all that. Just be in the state and hold it.

You can also let go of the ideas we derive
from the state: the soul (the thing that experiences it);
Angels (the beings who have attained the state's permanence);
and the Absolute (its ultimate extrapolation).

Just hold to the experience of the state. Promises
of abiding love, liberation from time, and congress
with higher worlds are yours to verify, not to believe.
Moses, Socrates, Jesus and Muhammad could be wrong.

The problem is that while entering the state is easy,
holding it is almost impossible. You'll start, proceed
some seconds, a minute, then fall out and reawaken
to it long later wondering what happened. Try again.

The present is in you to be found and experienced.
Once you've been here, whether you value its wonders enough
to make a life of it is your decision. Verify
everything. True God by any name is here now. Are you?

September 11

Still Breathing

You may think your body finished, but God still breathes in it.
It doesn't matter that you can't lift a pencil or pee
by yourself or that everyone is looking past your life.
Even if your very name flickers, God's presence abides.

The husk you're leaving behind is not you. Don't wait for it.
You must be very light – light itself – to cross God's threshold.
Call God but do not be the one calling. Be the presence,
be God becoming your full awareness, the nothing else.

September 12

Love

You might inquire what and where in all these poems is love.
The problem is I can't say any better than St. Paul
already has, or Petrarch, or Shakespeare, or whoever
first said God is love. We can examine what love is not –
that luscious delirium served on a bed of 'let us' –
but what it is and where in here to find it gives us pause.

You see, love and I cannot share a room. If love is here,
I must have departed, and if I preside, then the air
is unbreathable for love, so I cannot inform you
about love. Love is a state I can only imitate,
as I imitate real life, as God is imitating
everyone right now here: unmasking God, we'd disappear.

Let us just say when the Eye is open, love is the light
by which it sees. Call it God if you wish. I won't stop you.

September 13

The Host

The mind is a part of the body. The mind's resistance
to the truth, to simple being inviting God is seen
and felt in the muscles and nerves. That's why often in art
religious ecstasy is represented as a trance –
all the muscles gone slack, their patterned postures vacated –
or as a seizure – a conquering current projecting
the body into thrusted spasm, holy violence.

While experiencing God in these extremes is better
than not, better yet is the bright soul's open-armed welcome
following from the willed emptying of the mind and heart.
The soul's simple being is better company for God,
and the soul's control of mind and body extends to God
a tender hospitality. Don't make God neutralize
your mind just to visit you. Encourage the hosting soul.

September 14

Seeing God

Intelligent longing puts the house in order. The heart
must rise above its punier impulses – self-pity,
manic romance, pride in accomplishment – and turn its gaze
to the cloud over God's face with an acceptance stoic
and smoldering and an understanding that loving prayer
freely offered is sweeter than any self-indulgence.

To get ready to see God's face is to exhaust desire,
transforming from naïve seeker to embattled student
to subdued priest to empty vessel, open and offered
to creation. Even the mirror is a veil. Go through
and keep going. What is the last veil? When you are ready
to see God, you will be God, beyond all need of seeing.

September 15

Migration

When we speak of eternity, we mean a field of love
in which distance and spatial dimension have no meaning.
We can say the soul hovers above the sleeping body,
separated some for its own needed respiration,
but in truth its location is in neither time nor space.
And though the spirit, the light body, can, if the Angels
so will it, be glimpsed here on earth before our eyes fail us
and are overcome by the brightness, that body exists
as a discrete and unified being bridging all suns,
a sun unto itself. Even our amplest metaphors
dissolve at that border. Thus sadly malnourished is he
whose identity is this poor corpse, its language and thought.

Until we are by will united with the Absolute,
a condition we cannot conceive, the experience
of God is a movement of identity one level
beyond the current body, the weight we feel of ourselves.
For most of us now, that new level is love. God is love.
Give yourself to love and migrate to your welcoming soul.

September 16

Real

On one level, it's a play of forces: the more that will
can early recognize and resist imagination,
the more enticing the topics to be dismissed become.
The Sirens' probing music finds a weak spot in desire
to lure one in secret indulgence to the fatal rocks.

The will can't hold out indefinitely. We have one thing –
and one only – fixed in our favor. The presence of God
is sweeter than any lie and sweeter still the deeper
we breathe it and give our minds to it. This is another
way of saying God's love is real and incomparable.

The closet self that eats imagination's bait must have
your pity even as you starve it. It is what it is,
and that you know it is not God's love is your salvation.
Remembering God absolves the struggle that mortal flesh
would win by dying, taking you with it. God's love is real.

September 17

Old Enough

In the hollowing of age, we become ridiculous:
Don't fight back. Suffer the young's impatience and sneaky jokes.
Don't bring tired beauty back out for another feeble bow.
When memory won't return your calls, make no excuse.
Longing for the ground, the flesh sags and sallows. Let it go.

You're making progress. You've learned to be quiet and have lost
compunction about boring everybody. The slightest
breeze's kiss delights you more than the annual reunion.
You no longer send your friends regrets you don't really have.
All your resentment's gone. You've earned the right to surrender.

Release your old grip on time and let life have this moment
and the next. Attention is your soul's wordless poetry.
Even if your feet aren't moving, your dance of love summons
music from the whole galaxy. God's arms are open wide.

September 18

Our Children

The faculties for prophecy and poetry can't be
inherited. Peace and understanding can't be given.
What we can pass on is knowledge, reverence and delight,
and as we offer them through loving presence, we are right
to hope our children honor us and seek God for themselves.

But our children are not ours. They come through us on their way
to what they're making of their souls. Will the Angels help them?
As urgent as we are to ask that our children receive
what we have been given, it is better to practice peace
and try to understand whatever comes. Love them purely.

Are they not beautiful in their play of light and learning?
They have opened us. They have ransomed our hearts. Angels know
and we do not the balance each must pay to bring a soul
home to eternity. Take what's given. Pay all you can.

September 19

An End

A man with no esoteric education could slip
accidentally into a profound state of presence
and feel insane just from the luminous intensity
of perception. The shoppers in the aisles would be demons.

And a completed man crystallized in presence could not
help but be a bit apocalyptic in his worldview.
After all, things now move too fast for even the best minds
to keep the Great World Metaphor intact and functioning.

So it all comes apart – personality on one scale,
civilization on another. How to be ready?
Gather with your friends (the ones with whom presence can be shared)
and live above the flood: together you will be an Ark.

And if fire is the means of the end this time, the great flame
will be distributed among you all, so that each one
has a tiny tongue of it levitating from the Crown,
and you will know one language and share God with the Angels.

September 20

You

You've been pecking your way out for a year. It's time to hatch.
The universe is finally ready for you. Come forth!
Find your brothers and sisters, your partners in the present.
Make with them a high harmony of remembering God.
In the light of your beauty and the terror of your truth,
the world can't stay the same. You – all of you and more coming –
are the loving manifestation of understanding.
You bring eternity with you to renew the blessing.

September 21

Passing

Another day sinks from sight; the good deeds in this pen drain
their last syllables of love. Let's pretend the coming day
will be the last for us, that at some point our paths will split.
Does that make now different? The conundrum of using
time to be out of time transforms to poignant song as time
runs out. When I say I love you, I mean God is here. Look!
It is God coming to watch our attention. Where is yours?
Get the blessing that will make our parting like the passing
of a sacred lens between star gazers in the garden.

§ § §

www.ingramcontent.com/pod-product-compliance
Lightning Source LLC
Chambersburg PA
CBHW070346090426
42733CB00009B/1309